WHAT IF?

WHAT IF?

Joy was How you Measured
Success & the Money Proved
You Right!

Finola Howard

Book Interior and E-book Design by Amit Dey | amitdey2528@gmail.com

To find out more about our authors and books visit: www.intellectualperspective.com

TABLE OF CONTENTS

PRAISE FOR WHAT IF?

If you are a business owner who finds themselves wondering 'is this it?', this book is for you. It might be a short read but a long think! If my experience is anything to go by, you will find yourself stopping for some big ah-ha moments guided by the thoughtful exercises and the heartfelt prose.

Finola teases us steadily out of our business comfort zones drawing on her own experiences and those of her extensive client list. It is a call to arms but unusually for a business book the arms are the welcoming ones of finding joy in our business and purpose. I have a strong feeling reading this book will be a turning point for my business.

Dr Emma Williams,
Creatively Empowering Researchers in their Careers

I love this book! Finola's words have a way of challenging you in the best way to do more, believe more, and become more, not by becoming something you're not, but rather by becoming the person you were always meant to be. By listening to the whispers, nudges, and feelings deep inside of you and pushing through comfortable to instead have a purposeful business that brings joy. So much practical, intuitive, and sound business advice, that if followed will surely help the reader figure out exactly 'what they are for?'

Mary Farrelly, The Dog Knows,
Transforming the Way we Communicate with our Dogs

This book offers a new perspective on purpose and growth. Finola guides you through each step, so you can fully connect with what's important to you and set up your life in a way that gives you the best chance of achieving it. This isn't about hustle, it's growth on your own terms, in a way that's aligned with your values and most importantly brings you joy. And it's delivered with Finola's trademark compassion, humour and wisdom gained through years of experience. I couldn't put it down and can't wait to see the results I know it will bring.

Davina Ripton, Change Ready, Change Consultant,
Trainer, Mentor, Coach

'What If?' by Finola Howard is a special kind of book, one that combines deep personal reflection and insights with practical steps in how to develop a meaningful business from a place of joy. This book brings the reader on a journey, with a step by step process that encourages present and future business owners to name and claim their purpose not just as a way to generate wealth but long lasting fulfilment. Finola draws her wisdom into a new and innovative framework that I believe will enable all us entrepreneurs to discover and live our joy.

Rosemary Daynes Kearney, Founder of The Care Advocate,
GDPR Specialist, IRC Scholar

If you feel like I did, that you've let yourself drift from what brings you joy in your work, you need this inspiring and motivating read. It can sting a little to acknowledge the limitations you've been operating under by failing to use joy as a measure of success, but this book will provide the roadmap and reassurance you need to get back on track. A highly practical book that is much needed to help us all get our priorities back in alignment.

Frank Prendergast, Rise Above the Blah: AI Edition

FREE FOR YOU

There are many, many journals that went into the making of this book. Some I just had to place my hand over and I could remember where I was at that particular point in my journey. And then there were the conversations with people who each dropped a nugget that would lead me to where I wanted to be.

I believe in maps, in compasses and the freedom to choose whether it's time to wander or not. There should always be space for wandering. That's where the surprises come.

I've a little carry on for you to explore that will make this book all the richer. You will find it by signing up at www.toldandshared.com. In it you'll find:

Some Easy Listening
Some hand-picked podcast episodes of origin stories from idea, through the ups and downs and out the other side.

A second playlist of strategic tools and a third of some practical marketing techniques that you can use today. Still easy listening because there's always a story attached. I promise.

A Little Bit Of Fun

My log of ridiculousness. Stories of when you got told you were "too much". We laugh in the face of them here so that they will be banished forever.

Plans to make a working rocket because rocket science really is that easy!

Tools that Change Your Game

The **What If Canvas™** to stretch your brain and expand your limits.

The **Brand Inside** short course to help you transform the values you thought you had into behaviours that change the trajectory of your business.

The **Joy / Release Compass™** which will unlock your purpose and keep you moving from success to success in your business.

The **Business Joy Scale™** so you'll finally have metrics for joy in your business.

The **Proof in Numbers**, a series of case studies that show you how the numbers will prove that you were right to choose joy first.

All this, my friend is just a click away at www.toldandshared.com

WHAT IF – YOU ARE MY ONE READER?

The one that I wrote this story for. The entrepreneur who is amazing at what you do and yet you know you have the potential for more, perhaps even something great. But you've never unlocked it, and you're tired of being in that stuck place for far too long.

You want to know if fulfilling that unlocked potential of yours, is an adventure worth having at this point in your business and in your life. Or should you just be happy with where you are?

At the very least, this is an idea worth exploring. So, let's explore it together.

I still remember the day I started my business on 22 March 1999. It was my 30th Birthday and it was the day I chose to shape my working life from here on in. I left the perceived safety of employment as a marketing consultant to carve my own path. I was tired of the constraints, the second guessing and the inherent limits of having an employer who shapes your career, who decides how your work can feel every day and who also seems to define what you are worth.

It was a time of seismic change in the business world. A time when I was being asked by all the businesses I was working with: "Do you think this internet thing will ever catch on?" I did and I wanted to be part of it.

I took the leap and started a web design and marketing business with my then partner. Computer hardware was expensive at the time so we had to share our first one. I would use it during the day and he would use it at night.

It was annoying, but thankfully, we didn't have to do it for long because the business took off really quickly. I had already built a strong reputation for my strategic approach to marketing and I recognised that the internet was shaping the future for even the most established of businesses. There was a gap in the market for people like me who understood the impact that e-commerce was about to make in the world, and I grabbed it with both hands.

I still remember the clients who gave me my first break: Paul who wanted me to help his business build their first website and said, "Someone gave me a chance when I started; I want to do the same for you".

Emma, who not only hired me but recommended me to a local enterprise agency in the west of Ireland. I'll never forget the rigorous questioning by Frank, the CEO and we ultimately went on to spearhead a number of national initiatives that I am still proud of to this day.

David, who said, "We're kindred spirits, Finola; let's do this!" and is still a dear friend after all these years!

Such is the generosity of the people who become your customers. I have never forgotten them. They mark every stage of your business. They are the guides that come when you need them most and make way for the next ones as you take each leap.

I always know I'm growing when another guide shows up with something new for me to explore.

We never stop growing and we never grow alone.

We need those guides to show us what's next, what's possible and what else we can achieve.

They are the mirror of our potential and they serve to remind us that there is more to be done.

It is my hope that this book will be a guide for you – *if you are ready to come out of hiding at long last.*

Don't be offended. We all hide at some point in our lives and sometimes we don't even realise we're hiding until something or someone calls our attention to it, like I just have. It's actually quite normal.

Believe me when I say: you are ready to stop hiding. It's why you picked up this book.

You are ready to leave that place that feels like you are reaching for the stars, but not quite.

That place where you are touching your own potential but again, not quite.

It's there at the edge of your outstretched fingers, so close but just out of reach.

when you reach for
the stars

let go of the
tethers you make
for yourself

You can feel something tugging at your ankles and a restraint around your chest, restricting your heart. It stops you from that full stretch into your own potentiality, your own limitlessness and it feels like you're being cheated somehow.

It feels like someone teased you with your own possibility and left you holding on to a dream that would never be realised.

I invite you to shake it off, to grow through it, and embrace the fullness of who you are, to hear your own voice sharing your truth with the world as I am doing with this book.

I invite you to expand into YOU.

Yours in freedom

Finola x

SECTION 1

SO, WHAT ARE YOU AFRAID OF ANYWAY?

You know what it means to walk with fear beside you, to use it as a catalyst and transform it into excitement. You've had as many discomfort zones as comfort zones. But this discomfort is a little different, isn't it? This one is all about truly being vulnerable. Being vulnerable enough to show your full self; the one you haven't fully met yourself yet because you've buried them so deep. You dream of it, but it's still a little hazy. You feel it in your soul, but you've never fully looked at it in the mirror.

It's time now. You see those around you overtaking you. Some are younger, some less experienced, some have even been your students. You are happy for them, but you find yourself asking: how come they've been able to reach their potential, taking their business to the next level, and you haven't?

It's time to get past those last few blocks and finally do it.

Here's the reassuring bit for you: this feeling that you are feeling is more common than you think. It's a rite of passage for all of us in business. And while it is true that we must each take our own steps on this path, take comfort in the knowledge that you are not the only one who will walk it.

I offer this book to you as a guide to accompany you on this next stage of your journey. A guide through the limiting self-talk that you can choose to poke at and reframe for yourself. Not sure if you need a guide? Okay, here are three statements I heard myself say at one point in my life and they have been echoed by so many other entrepreneurs I've met or worked with over the years. Do you see yourself in any of these?

1. I'm not sure I even want the success that I know is possible for me.
2. I'm afraid that I might have to compromise who I am to get it.
3. I'm just one person. How could I possibly make a difference in the world?

But you can make that difference and you are meant to make it.

We are all meant to.

1: DO YOU EVEN WANT SUCCESS?

There's a place between success and failure that is so seductive it's almost impossible to leave. We call it the "comfort zone". It's a place where there is "just enough" but doesn't quite get you all the way there.

Things are relatively easy in this place but you find yourself having the same conversations again and again. There is comfort in being the expert but there's nothing really new here.

Yes, it's efficient, you're consistent and your revenue is consistent too even if it does come in waves. That doesn't bother you too much because you know there will always be another wave coming your way soon.

You're quite used to this level of success.

But you don't quite get the same kick out of it that you once did.

You start to think to yourself – is this it?

Is this what you worked so hard for all this time?

Has it been worth all the effort?

Has it been worth the long hours of travel, the missed moments, the self-doubt, the tiredness, the keeping going when others would have given up?

But then something whispers at the back of your mind.

You lean in a little to let yourself hear it.

Hear the Whisper

It will be worth it, you know... If you're willing to go the rest of the way. You can do more with your life. You can have more. You're just there.

And then, you'll finally know what it feels like to have given it your best shot. To have reached your full potential and not to have any regrets. This is your chance. Will you take it?

Will you take a chance on the YOU, you were meant to be?

The YOU who sees all your dreams realised, who stands on that stage and owns it, who is financially abundant and living in joy, in peace and in flow?

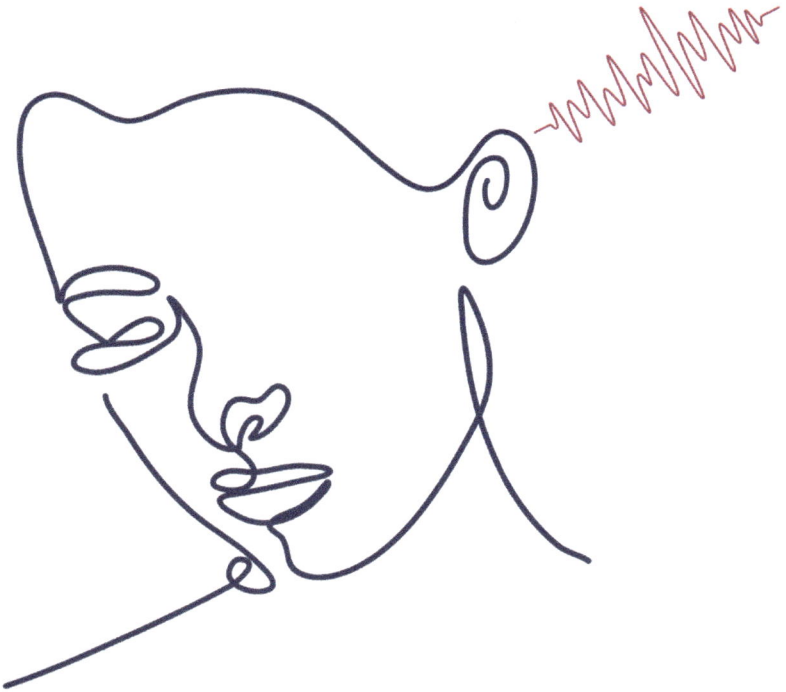

hear the whisper...

Success Is Not A Passive Endeavour

You have to actively choose it. Choosing it means you get to decide the shape of it. What it looks like, how it feels, who you engage with, what you work on and for how long, what the rewards look like; in terms of time, money, health, wellbeing – all of these things. And until you decide on the shape of your success, it will never be yours.

You may have fallen into the trap that there's only one formula to success.

That's true. There is. Your formula. Your decision to make.

Hustle is not a prerequisite. Burnout is not an obligation. Nor is visibility without boundaries.

You choose. Nobody else.

Success does not require sacrifice. It does not have to come at a price you are not willing to pay.

> *"Success is liking yourself, liking what you do,*
> *and liking how you do it."*
>
> – Maya Angelou

Feel into that quote from Maya Angelou. Sit with it a moment. See how there needs to be a connection with yourself, with what you do and how you do it? There must be harmony between all three. That sets the ground rules for your personal definition of success.

This version of success is not a destination or an "end point". That's where we get confused. We're fooled into thinking that "some day, I'll be successful enough to feel like this".

The true possibility is that we can feel like this now. This is our desired state of being as opposed to our destination. When that colours our state of mind, it permeates all our thinking and our decisions. It becomes in effect a true compass point for what we want.

What you "want" is critical. Because "want" is where growth happens.

Want moves you beyond "need" where "just enough" maintains the status quo and limits possibilities.

Need is easier because you **have** to do it so it's never really about you.

In contrast "want" is absolutely about you. It's where you have to move your focus to you.

Nobody else, not your partner, your children, your parents, your friends, your peers – You.

Want is more challenging because you must actively choose it. So, here's the question:

How do you teach yourself to want?

I have to admit, I always found this difficult; this idea of wanting for myself.

I used to feel like it was a little self-indulgent. That there was nothing grand or of a higher purpose about wanting for yourself, was there? That old conditioning of "who am I to want something more?"

You would be surprised how often I've heard that in the clients who have come to me over the years.

The Marianne Williamson quote always sprang to mind

"Our deepest fear is not that we are inadequate. Our deepest fear is that we are powerful beyond measure. It is our light, not our darkness that most frightens us. We ask ourselves, 'Who am I to be brilliant, gorgeous, talented, fabulous?' Actually, who are you not to be?"

And yet, I didn't quite walk that path myself. Some ideas I could internalise intellectually and even embrace from a spiritual perspective, and yet, until I lived them, I couldn't quite believe them.

Here's where I remind you that "want" is growth; your growth.

This is about working from a higher vibration, a more positive state. Building a resonance with your own possibilities. You are actively moving beyond need, beyond the oxygen mask analogy which is simply not enough. The oxygen mask is about survival whereas what you really want is to flourish.

"Wanting" in this context is about actively seeking a positive desired state.

That positivity not only signals flourishing, it also produces flourishing.[1]

You want to flourish for yourself; for your own growth and wellbeing and for the difference you want to make in the world.

This is about fulfilling your potential, nobody else's.

When you're learning how to want, start with the impossible

Choose something big. Choose something that seems impossible or impractical.

A few years ago, my partner Kevin and I bought a camper van at the end of the summer holidays.[2] It was a whim. I'd never been in a camper van before but Kevin loved them and knew them. Why not! It was a way to have an adventure.

We bought an older camper van, one we could do up and flip if we didn't like it. We took a couple of weekend trips away to get the feel of her. And one night, over a few glasses of wine, we started to imagine what if we took off on a rambling tour of France for three months during the summer.

All the rationalisations reared their heads. How could Kevin take three months off work? How could I take three months off from my business? But the brain is a beautiful thing.

What if suddenly transformed into "why not"!

So, we tapped into Kevin's previously unused parental leave and kitted the van out with everything I'd need to do a little work, if I needed to, and we booked the ferry. We didn't know if we could do it. We thought it was ridiculous but we did it anyway.

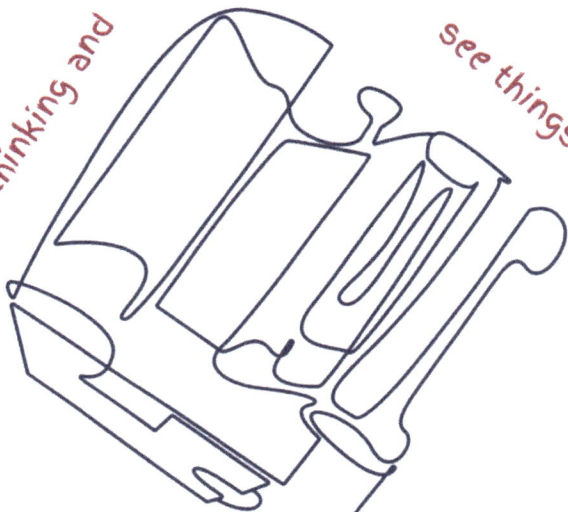

Flip your thinking and see things from a new perspective

And what an adventure we had! We didn't plan it. We each picked the places we wanted to see and then we wandered in between them all discovering new places as we went.

We landed in Carcassonne the day before the Tour de France came through, and we cheered the peloton up front and centre before they departed. The following night was Bastille Day and Carcassonne has the second-largest fireworks display in all of France, after Paris. They are set off over the whole mediaeval city and it was amazing to see. We even bumped into some campers from Cork and shared a few glasses of vino with them.

We got lost trying to find the famous Lascaux caves and laughed when Sean (age 6) piped up to say, "Oh they moved where you visit them years ago – you need to go to Lascaux II." Apparently, they'd duplicated the caves so the original ones wouldn't deteriorate any more from exposure to the air people were breathing there when they visited.

We visited the submarine pens in Saint Nazaire and got stuck on the side of a mountain in a campsite called Namaste and ate perfectly cooked steak in a lightning storm. We got lost in an underground roundabout in Monte Carlo and headed over the Alps to Castellane, a town with a deep history of resistance fighters from World War II and we got to hear the stories.

This trip was a mindset shift for us. It taught us that anything is possible. It taught us how to think differently. To shake off what is conventionally possible and just do it.

I learned that you have to take action to make the impossible possible.

And you start by teaching yourself to want it.

When you teach yourself that, you realise that there is nothing you cannot have, do, or accomplish.

Hear the Whisper

I see you there in that place where you've done it. You imagined something nobody else would have done. It seemed so big and possibly too big for so many. But you broke it down so you could see how to make it happen.

You didn't leave it to someone else to do. You did it.

Feed the Whisper

Pick something that you **want** to have, to accomplish or to feel. Make it a stretch, even a small one. Something that right now, feels a little impossible. Break it down. Get really pragmatic about it. What are the steps to getting this done? Embrace "what if" and "why not".

Make a plan. Then do it. Then do it again for something else.

Get used to wanting and getting.

Then, do it again.

When You Know Why You Want It, You'll Leap

When our son Sean was just three years old, I placed him in the back of the car to bring him to his grandmother's for the day. I could see his chubby little face in the rear-view mirror as he stared out the window wistfully. And I smiled to myself. He was happy and so I was happy too. Then he asked me this question:

What are you for, Mammy?

Very early on, as parents, we made a decision to always answer Sean's questions as best we could. I'd gotten caught out before when he asked me about the reason for different sized buckets on a digger but that's another story. I should have known better, but I suppose I wasn't expecting this one.

I stuttered and I stumbled and came up with some answer I "*thought*" I should give.

Mm uhh... I'm here to love you sweetheart...

He smiled but I could tell he wasn't that impressed. I knew the minute I said it, that it wouldn't be enough. Frustrated, I asked the same question in return, thinking I'd stump him. Not a chance! Without a stumble or a pause for breath, he answered:

I'm for digging!

I laughed, wowed by his clarity, and I complimented him for his certainty. We chatted away about his favourite types of diggers for the rest of the trip. He just came alive speaking about them. They were one of his first passions and he always embraces his passions.

Sean continues to be a source of inspiration for me in a way that always stops me in my tracks.

And here's the truth of it.

We need to be stopped in our tracks!

There is too much time spent on hamster wheels. Doing things that we think we "should" be doing just because everyone else is doing them or talking about doing them. "Should" is the enemy of true growth. It's a distraction from what will move the needle in your business and what is simply someone else's priority.

Here's the thing: I believe fundamentally that we are all here with purpose.

It's a position I take quite seriously and it underpins all the work I do. Unfortunately, as with most overused terms, "purpose" has lost all meaning. It is something that makes people's eyes glaze over, yawn and skip to the end of the chapter or move onto the next person they have to listen to at a networking event.

And yet, every story of success starts with purpose.

It's the moment all business owners realise why they are here and what they're going to do about it.

Mick Kelly, founder of GIY, started a global movement of sustainably grown food because the bulb of garlic he picked up in the supermarket was shipped to Ireland all the way from China. It opened his eyes about the food sector and made him ask the question "Why are we importing something from more than 8,000 km away when it can be grown perfectly here?"

David Walsh and Niall Kelly started global security firm Netwatch because their friend was attacked while responding to a workplace alarm. Together, they felt there had to be a better way to protect property and, more importantly, first responders. They discovered a company in Australia that specialised in military transmission technology for military installations, jumped on a plane to Melbourne and Netwatch was born.

Brendan O'Hara and Kendal Parmar started Untapped as a way of taking all the data that we collect and using AI to give it back to us in a way that will help us learn more about ourselves; democratising self-awareness, preventing burnout and driving real organisational change.

I have so many stories like this. I collect them in the conversations I have with clients and guests on my podcast.

You can listen to their stories in a curated series of my podcast episodes here. I've also included an episode of my own origin story too.

www.toldandshared.com

We are all offered our own reason for being in the world.

You will hear it when you stop to listen for it. We are given clues as to its nature our whole lives.

And our lives are set up in a way that gives us the best chance to achieve that purpose. The challenges we face at each turn teach us the skills we need to accomplish that purpose. The opportunities we are offered show us what's possible for each leap forward. It's why we meet the people we need to meet at every stage.

Purpose is a gift. It is the most important gift you will ever choose to receive.

It is tied to that which you want for yourself and that is why only you can receive it.

Many people choose not to receive it.

Sometimes consciously. Sometimes unconsciously.

Perhaps, the idea of "purpose" comes with a sense of too much responsibility.

Something else you "have" to do.

What if, instead, purpose was a means of producing joy? Your joy?

That as you move closer and closer towards expanding into it, you are rewarded with joy?

That has been my experience.

The converse is also true.

The further I am from my own purpose, the unhappier I am.

your purpose is a gift

of joy to you

receiving it is optional

So, what are <u>you</u> for?

As we search for purpose, it is often difficult to pinpoint the moment it was born. It is only in retrospect that the "origin story" becomes clear.

There are, however, lots of signposts along the way. Moments where your passion is ignited and you speak out about something, or want to innovate how you approach a problem that needs to be solved, or connect all your insights in a way that isn't being done.

Think back to those moments. They are individual story moments that point you to purpose. Write them down. Don't attach yourself to them. Just trust those moments are trying to tell you the story of your purpose.

You need this story. It's what will sustain you when things are tough. It will sustain you as you take your next leap between who you are now to who you are becoming.

Receive the gift of your purpose and run with it.

Hear the Whisper

Remember that time you got so frustrated over that situation... And the other time you were so sad because of what happened to that person you met. You knew there could be a better way... A way that you could fix. And then there was the time you felt so in your element, so natural, so filled with a sense of rightness that here in this moment you were in the right place, at the right time, doing the right thing.

Feed the Whisper

Feel into each of these moments. These are the signs. See them for what they are.

Piece them together and know that you are here with purpose.

And if you feel brave enough, feel into what it would be like to choose it.

To choose to receive that gift of purpose and run with it.

Choose The Shape Of Your Success And Become It

Have you noticed that something is already taking shape for you now. It's the shape of the life and business that you choose for you. Yes, it's probably a little fuzzy still around the edges, but we can fix that to see it clearly without any limits so you can lay claim to it.

You know the power of wanting something now. It's deeply connected to your own growth. You also know that what you want is connected to your purpose.

The next step is to BECOME it in order to LIVE it. And you can't BECOME it until you see it clearly.

Let me ask you: how do you *"see"* things? Do you see in pictures, in words, in making something with your hands? Do you see in sound?

It's best to take all the ways so you can create a sensory overload for your own success.

Then you'll really start to believe in it.

Take some time to play here. Be literal AND use metaphors.

Journal the shape of your success
Write the story of what the shape of your unique success is like. Write it in the present tense so it's not some far distant future and you can already get a glimpse of it. Add a richness to the language as you describe it so you'll know what it looks like and feels like and you won't pass it by on the journey to get there. You'd be surprised how many entrepreneurs pass by their own mile markers of success without enjoying each one of them. What kind of adventure can success really be if you don't stop to enjoy it along the way.

Walk in the shoes of your own success
I remember a course I took, many years ago, where we wrote anchor words on small pieces of paper and placed

them in our shoes and walked with them every day for thirty days. They started as minor annoyances under our feet calling us to remember that we walked in shoes of freedom, of abundance, of joy until they simply became part of us and the pieces of paper themselves disappeared.

It was an exercise in "becoming", in physically absorbing an idea into who you are. So, as you take each step, knowing each word is in your shoe, you start to "take in" the idea that this is who you are.

It was a powerful, daily reminder of something I wanted to internalise. I could feel the connection being made with every step until it became who I was, standing taller as I walked in the knowledge that something important had happened.

Colour Your Success. Use paints or crayons to create this picture. Alternatively buy a piece of art that captures it. Put it somewhere you can see it every day. What colours express your success best? Is there a picture forming? What does it look like? Can you see yourself in that picture even metaphorically? Can you feel it? Does it make you smile?

Build it in Lego.[3] Sometimes our hands know the truth of something before we do. Lego discovered this for themselves when they were dissatisfied with the way their own strategy sessions were going so, they created a way to unlock creativity in their business and called it Lego Serious Play. They understood that when you build you make new knowledge and you can never be done building because that would mean you knew everything. Why not build your idea of success with Lego. Allow your hands to guide you and help you imagine what your success looks like physically. Build in metaphor. That's where the magic happens. If you are too literal here you won't activate your imagination and that's what we want, your imagination in action.

Add sound. It could be the rustle of something, or a recording of you laughing. It could be a song that reaches you deep inside and triggers that feeling of success you want to feel. You might find yourself dancing in your living room or belting out a ballad to a hairbrush. You could be recording the intro to your own radio show or podcast that you want to launch. It could be the sound of applause after you've spoken at an event or the ringing of a bell because you just landed that contract. I've worked in several companies where we always rang the bell when we landed a contract. Whatever allows you to take your own success in, to embrace it fully into who you are.

Add taste. Is it champagne? A good risotto? A strawberry? A glass of Guinness? What is it for you? Taste it. Does it feel luxurious, simple, organic, messy? Is it something you'd eat somewhere warm or cold? Is it associated with a place? Take yourself there.

Add smell. Is it lavender on a hot day in the south of France? The smell of the sea in the middle of the day? The leather seats in a new car? Is it sweet like they say? Would you believe they've done research on this and it seems success smells of patchouli but it's got to be blended with something else too. For men, it's got to be blended with sandalwood or spicy black pepper. For women, it needs to be mixed with tropical fruits or floral scents. [4]

Add touch. Is it a swim in the ocean, feeling the freedom of the expanse of the sea around you? I know that is one of mine. The freedom that there are no limits to where I can go. The abundance that I feel being part of something so vast and so powerful. The ease of movement in my body which again teaches me about freedom. The realisation that I'll get to where I want to go by moving with the flow and not against it. Testing my own limits by swimming all year round in different types of weather like rain, snow, hale, cold, warmth, and sun.[5] The embrace of the sea on my skin. The simple joy of that. I have found so many metaphors in the sea for my own journey; it is a constant source of inspiration for me.

This is about embracing success in a way that you can BECOME it in the present moment.

So you can access it whenever you need.

So you can get comfortable with it.

So that it BECOMES you.

Hear the Whisper

You were meant to get comfortable with this feeling of success.

It's your most natural state.

Get used to it.

More of it is coming.

Feed the Whisper

Create a space in your space.

A physical space that embodies success for you.

Fill it with what success feels like for you.

Use all the senses you've been exploring it with in this chapter.

Allow yourself to become that feeling in this space you've created for yourself.

And as you sit and take it all in, realise that you are already here.

ENDNOTES

1.   Fredrickson BL. *The role of positive emotions in positive psychology. The broaden-and-build theory of positive emotions.* Am Psychol. 2001 Mar;56(3):218-26. doi: 10.1037//0003-066x.56.3.218. PMID: 11315248; PMCID: PMC3122271.

2.   Love of my life and father to our son Sean.

3.   Listen to my podcast episode chatting with Per Kristiansen, one of the original master trainers in Lego Serious Play and author of *Building a Better Business Using the Lego Serious Play Method.*

4.   *Creston : Scent-sational new study reveals the real smell of success* - March 2014:https://www.marketscreener.com/quote/stock/CRESTON-PLC-4002034/news/Creston-Scent-sational-new-study-reveals-the-real-smell-of-success-18160399/

5.   Always swimming safely and never alone.

2: ARE YOU TOO SMALL TO HAVE A BIG PURPOSE?

One of the things I've always been proud of is seeing the difference my work makes to the lives and businesses of my clients. It is a source of great joy for me. And yet as time moved on and I started to move through these stages that you are reading right now, I started to wonder about my own possibilities. I started to wonder "what if" for myself.

That's where the whisper you're becoming familiar with was born.

Something started to happen to that whisper and a scarier idea was starting to emerge:

What if that voice, I kept pushing to the side,
stopped whispering because
I'd waited too long?

It was like a punch to the stomach and this is when my own journey started to turn up a notch and I finally made the decision to go for it.

Don't Let The Magic Of Your "What If" Voice Disappear

"What If" is the voice of possibility and potential.

"What If" holds the key to your purpose in this world.

It is your inner wisdom that knows who you already are on the inside, just waiting for you to manifest on the outside. It's the voice of your own growth and it needs to be nourished with positivity so you can achieve your potential.

You want your "what if" voice to grow beyond your fears and doubts and beyond the cacophony of the world outside. Beyond the ones who want to keep you safe, beyond the ones who wish it was them, beyond the ones who are comfortable with where you are now.

Make it loud so you can hear it. Help it grow beyond a whisper.

Because until you hear this voice clearly, nobody is going to hear yours.

Start your mornings with "What If"

Give it a voice in the bathroom mirror. Say it out loud in the car. Feed the shape of your potential with your voice first. The one that you are starting to hear emerge more clearly now.

- What if I could stand on a stage and hold them all in the palm of my hands?
- What if I could change their lives with just my words?
- What if I didn't have to work so hard?

- What if I was mortgage free?
- What if I didn't have to do everything in person?
- What if I could build something that gave them power over their own health?
- What if I could solve the clean water challenge in certain countries?
- What if I could make them smile again?
- What if...

The more you play with your "what if" voice, the more you will find yourself also answering the "what are you for" question with a clearly stated purpose. The clearer you state your purpose, the more your entrepreneurial brain will naturally start to see <u>how</u> you can achieve it.

Hold off on that "how" step for a while because when you move into "how" you will stop imagining "What If" and it's too soon for that yet. We want you imagining an impossible future because nobody will imagine it quite like you do. Nobody will have your perspective.

When you move to "how" you will have left imagination and impossibility. Practicality will have taken root and it's too soon for that yet.

You have to stay long enough in "purpose" to make sure your leap isn't too small.

Purpose is not found in the shuffle.
It's built in the leap.

– Finola Howard

Purpose is not found in the shuffle.

It's built in the leap.

Finola Howard

Be mindful of the entrepreneurial tendency to get purpose and mission (how) mixed up[1]. As entrepreneurs we always default to how. We just want to get things done. For true growth to occur you need the magic of "What If" to inform your purpose. It's got to feel big enough that you don't quite know how you'll pull it off.

If it feels a little "howish", then you've probably jumped into your natural tendency to get things done and have actually focused in on your mission.

I remember working with a company who spent a significant amount of time on what they believed was their "purpose". They really stretched themselves as a leadership team and were proud of what they'd framed for themselves for the future. And yet, I could see action in their words and knew they'd defaulted to how and not why.

So, we did an exercise and we moved what they'd written for purpose into the section underneath that I'd created for mission. I asked them to consider the possibility that what they'd written was a statement of how (mission) and not purpose (why). I asked them to "chunk up", to go bigger and see what the "mission" they'd just written could deliver on. What purpose (why) could that accomplish?

That's when it got real.

I remember Paul[2], the team lead sharing how emotional and vulnerable he felt as he articulated a possible purpose for the business.

He was almost whispering this purpose because it felt so personal and so true to who he was as a human being. A truth that others around the table were nodding in agreement to with similar expressions on their faces.

And then I knew we'd done it. This is what they were here for.

This is what their purpose was in the world.

An unapologetic statement when once uttered out loud starts to gather power behind it.

It gathers power because it is believable.

It is believable because it's true.

This is what would dictate their true trajectory.

It did and it has.

Remember this: if you don't "feel it", it's not your true purpose.

I've made this Purpose, Mission, Vision exercise available to you in www.toldandshared.com

Feel the Whisper

It's not enough to hear me, you've got to feel me too.

I've got to take up space in your whole body.

You'll know it's yours because it'll feel so true.

You can finally realise what you are here to do.

Feed the Whisper

When you're choosing what you're here for, feel into it. Wait for a reaction somewhere in your body: your gut, your heart, your shoulders. Listen to what your body is telling you.

Trust it. Then act on it.

Build Yourself A What If Canvas

As the whisper gets louder, a war may ensue. It's the war between your higher self; the voice of your own freedom, the one we've been tuning into, and your small self, who is trying to keep you safe. Your small self is the place where imposter syndrome likes to hang out but we don't want to hang out there any more.

So we've got to make sure we capture everything we've discovered so far.

We need to take that voice we've been feeding and get it on paper so you can't talk yourself out of it.

Get a big sheet of paper – it's got to be at least A3 in size.

And a big marker too. It's got to take up space. No small writing here.

Big and loud, an unencumbered higher self; that's what we want.

At the top of the sheet write "MY WHAT IF CANVAS".

Remember your morning ritual at the start of this chapter? It's time to take those ideas that have only been expressed verbally up until now and commit them to paper.

The only rules here are

1. Every sentence needs to start with "What If".
2. Every sentence must be positive.

And let loose. Explore the possibilities. Think expansively.

Fill the page. Then fill another.

Keep going until you stop.

"What If" banishes imposter syndrome because you don't have to justify "What If".

"What If" is not a decision that needs explanation.

"What If" is an exploration of possibilities.

"What If" taps directly into you.

Feel the Whisper

That's it. You're doing it.

Let it come.

It's the truth of who you are meant to be.

Let it come.

Tune In To You, Then Choose

I've come to appreciate the different dimensions to the people I've met over the years. It's made me appreciate my own and not to worry about justifying them.

I have a side that loves the pragmatic, the process and getting things done. I like the step by step and the worksheet. I like to create the boxes then step out of them. That's where the juicy stuff lives.

There's another side of me that's deeply intuitive, which I trust. I trust it because it feels like "truth". My clients smile when they see me do it. I sit into where I am, two feet on the ground, rooted to the moment. I listen in. And I wait. I tend to look up to my left as I listen in. My clients know the signal, so they wait too.

We all wait for the truth to come.

It always comes.

The thing is, this is not unique to me. This is a capability that every one of us has and we each have our own way of accessing it.

Let's tune into yours

This is not a head exercise

It's a body exercise

Start by grounding yourself. Sit with both feet on the ground and get quiet. Tune into your body. Think of this as a listening pose. Feel where your truth lives. Place your hand there and anchor that feeling. Stay there a while so you realise the importance of this moment. The moment when you know where the home of your truth lives.

If the idea of sitting into this deep listening pose is new to you, you'll need to give yourself a minute or two to really feel this. This is not a head exercise. This is a body exercise. We are not in the intellect here. Don't read on, until you are truly grounded and are ready to listen with your body.

Make sure your "What If" Canvas™ is close at hand, the one you've just been building, and with something bright (a coloured marker, a highlighter) allow yourself to be guided to those ideas that fill you up. That you feel in your body. Don't do anything unless you feel it in your body.

Banish any thoughts of why something is "not possible", thoughts around "should" or anything practical here.

Light up the words that light you up.

Light them up with colour.

These are the truths of where you want to be. Trust them.

Then choose them.

The act of choosing will always come first.

This is your "vision" piece. This is what your success looks like.

Success that you've chosen for yourself.

Feel the Whisper

Trust yourself to choose what's right for you.

You'll feel it in your body when you've found it.

ENDNOTES

1. Episode #47 Why Purpose, Mission and Vision Matter; Your Truth Shared
2. Actual names are protected.

3: WHEN YOU GET THERE, WILL YOU STILL BE YOU?

As you tune in to hear yourself and what you want, you'll get excited at the possibilities that are opening up for you. You'll feel the expansion not only in your mind but also in your body.

When you're being positive, this will feel like a natural inclination to take up space in the world and it's a powerful thing. It's also a little disconcerting. It's something different and it always takes us a while to adjust to this new feeling before it becomes our new normal. Keep that idea with you.

Remind yourself that this is your new normal.

This is also the moment where self-sabotage can find the crack and weasel its way in. You may find yourself looking around at people ahead of you on this path and see what you "think" they've had to do to build the success they've wanted. It seems like they're single minded, sometimes even ruthless or they're, "always on" and have built large teams around them to get to where they are. You don't know what road they've taken and you'll probably never know. But they will have been where you are now and faced the same fundamental choices you are facing now. And they will have chosen.

This is the moment when you realise that if you truly commit to this path then you'll have to make some significant changes. Changes; not just to your business, but to you, yourself as a person.

And the self-sabotage crack just got wider.

keep going

it will heal itself

So, take a pause. Notice that this is happening. Know that you can prepare for it by simply being aware that this is what happens to everyone at this stage. It's the moment where you have the choice to stop reading this book and go back to where you were. It's safer there, isn't it?

But is it? When was "safe" ever really that safe? When was holding yourself back from realising your full potential ever a viable option? When was it ever enough?

So breathe. Long deep breaths to quiet the turbulence.

Breathe in for 4. Hold for 4.

Breathe out for 4. Hold for 4.

And again.[1]

It has always amazed me how powerful breathwork is. It is a tool that can move you through deep change and one you can tap into at any moment. This is the tool you need in this moment.

The tool you can use to normalise your expansiveness, breathing into it and moving through.

Breathing into it and becoming the real you.

The "You" You Are Now Is Not You At All

The "real you" doesn't have limits. The real you has imagination and choice in equal measure.

This is the YOU you were meant to be.

The YOU that you are free to be now.

Yes, this is unknown and uncharted space. It is a step towards joy.

The joy of being YOU.

And yet, sometimes "joy" is scarier than the alternative.

But that alternative has already been conquered. It is the status quo where you "think" you've got it all under control. Where, in fact, this lesser version of yourself is controlling you and keeping you there.

Keeping you in a "half self".

It's become so normalised for you now, that you've accepted it as who you are.

And that's just not true.

"What If" is your friend here.

"What If" will show you that joy is the better option.

Even if it is a little scary.

A long, long time ago in a different version of myself. I was in a relationship[2] of fourteen years that was steadily deteriorating as my definition of normality moved little by little, eating away at me. Very few people knew it was a bad relationship and extracting myself from it was difficult and took a very circuitous route.

If I do this, will it be different? No. What about this? No. Or this? No. This kept repeating until I had to draw some line in the sand that I couldn't move past. So, I gave myself a deadline to make a decision, either way. I arranged to go on a retreat to Sedona in Arizona and I would make the decision there. In the meantime, I just put my head down and worked. I didn't worry about what the outcome was until I went on my retreat. There I would make my choice.

It was a powerful experience as you can imagine. What was most powerful was the time spent hearing myself, tuning into the truth that I knew deep inside. I had to leave. So, I did.

But this is not the point of my story. This was not the most difficult choice I had to make. This, I had prepared myself for. What I hadn't realised was what it would feel like to be alone. Buying for one. Coming home to an empty house. Walking the dog we had cared for together. Free of the stress of that co-dependent relationship. Free to be me.

Realising that I had a limitless freedom to choose whatever I wanted next.

I hadn't thought that far ahead and when I did, my mind would go blank with possibility.

And then he reached out. I don't even remember the details or the promises.

I just remember this. A moment in the shower where I was on this knife edge decision point. Do I go back? I know what that looks like. I can navigate that. I know the variables. It's so familiar, it's so tempting. It would be easy, wouldn't it?

The choice

is always
yours to make

And this other option. That could be filled with joy. But what does joy look like? That's completely unknown. I don't know how to be there. I don't know how to live there. It's really scary. How would I be in that life? What would I be in that life? Do I know that person? No. I don't.

But…? It was a silent "What If". Not yet articulated.

And in that moment I leapt.

I chose joy.

I've never regretted it.

My life transformed with that decision.

Because joy is <u>always</u> the better option.

I share this story here, with purpose.

This is not about the choice to end a difficult situation.

It is about the difficult choice to live in a new way.

To face the unknown trusting that it's better than the status quo.

I bet you know what that feels like. To feel utterly alone in that choice.

To wonder if it's the right choice.

When I look back at that version of me, the woman who made that choice, I'm forever grateful for the leap she took. I'm forever grateful for the courage it took to choose the unknown.

To choose the possibility of joy. It wasn't certain then. It was only a possibility.

But even the possibility of joy is always the better option.

So this is my question for you. What decision will you make?

Will you choose to stay in comfort, in this diluted version of your potential?

Or will you choose to leap, to embrace the possibilities that choosing joy can bring?

Do you choose this next version of yourself?

The YOU you were meant to be?

I truly hope you do.

Your Values Will Shape The New You

Real values are not random words chosen on a whim to satisfy a tick box exercise.

They are a clear declaration of what you stand for.

They are felt in the heart and in the soul.

They are behaviours that you live by and stick to, even when they are tested.

> *Real values are actionable and that means they can be measured.*
>
> – Finola Howard

You uncover them by looking inward first.

As you step into them you will find yourself looking outward and upward.

And in doing so, you are inadvertently setting your own trajectory from this point.

Try it. You cannot play small with values that demand your action.

They come from the very best part of you.

And as such they are uniquely yours.

In all my years of working on values in this way with my clients, I have yet to meet anyone whose values are expressed in the same way. Here's a few that might inspire you:

__Julie Silfverberg,__ a powerful NLP coach turned website builder, made her primary value "__Have Fun Making Hard Choices__". This is her third successful business and she wanted to ensure that, at this point in her life, everything she did would be fun. She wanted that to be the same experience for her clients too; so much so, she built it into how she works.

__Michelle Hone and Sarah Kelly__, female scientists, and co-founders of supplements company __HEROLOGY™ The Science of HER,__ wanted to change the narrative in women's healthcare that has traditionally led us to believe that suffering at the mercy of hormonal irregularities and fluctuations was something that women just needed to "get on with". Their first two values are "__Celebrate What It Means To Be A Woman__" and "__Develop Products That Actually Work for Women__".

Niamh O'Callaghan, *Interior Designer and Founder of* **Tigh Design: Creating Spaces That Speak of You,** *believes we can learn to slow down by being purposeful and intentional about how we consume and what we incorporate into our homes for its sentimentality and functionality. Her first two values are* "**Feel The Beauty With All The Senses**" *and* "**Find the Flow in Function To Make the Home Work**".

Tina O'Dwyer, *Founder of* **The Tourism Space,** *a specialist sustainable tourism consultancy who partners with government and the public sector to help reframe what success in tourism means today, by taking a place centred approach and enabling a better future for people and places through tourism. While their work is international they have embraced their own place in the world with values expressed in the Irish language including* "**Meitheal – Facilitate collective effort for greater good**" *and* "**Misneach – Be brave, spirited and ambitious for better**".

Mary Jennings, *Founder of* **Forget The Gym: Go Outside. Get Moving. Feel Alive**. *believes getting outside can make you feel energised, enthusiastic and calmer in the rest of your life. Her primary values are* "**Create Freedom Experiences**" *and* "**Make It Simple**".

Here's one of mine:

> **Look for the Joy** – *it's the greatest measure of how we know we are doing the right work. It also means we are committed to making the experience a joyful one for everyone we work with. That means there is mutual respect, trust and a collaborative space where co-creation thrives.*

This is such a strong navigation point for me. When I don't feel the joy or the potential for joy in my work, I know now to tune in to feel what's going on and adjust my present course of action. It is a powerful tool for my own growth.

Are you ready for it to be your turn?

To declare for yourself what you stand for?

To set your own trajectory, knowing you're on the right course.

The first step is to choose the values you will live by in this business of yours.

It starts by tuning into the words that you feel in your gut. You feel them because they matter.

And because they matter they have the potential to push you further, to be better and to serve better.

When you do that, the trajectory of your success rises just that bit higher because you are that bit better. Do not underestimate their power.

You can call them to mind, use a dictionary or you can use the suggestions I've included in The Brand Inside minicourse I've created for you. You can access it and download it from www.toldandshared.com and start tuning in.

When you've downloaded the list, move through each word, one at a time, feel into them, and choose the twenty words that resonate most with you. Tick each one as you go. Don't forget to stop at twenty.

The first pass through is always quicker; you're just looking for a spark of recognition.

The next time as you whittle those twenty back to ten spend a little longer.

Which ten do you feel more? Give them a second tick so you acknowledge that you've actively chosen them.

One last pass, and this one has to count.

Your final choice is five words that matter to you; five words that conjure up stories of meaning to you. Feel them and you will be rewarded with your own truth.

These five words are your starting point.

I remember doing this exercise in 2016, a few months before my dad was taken into hospital in his final stages of Parkinson's. I didn't know what lay ahead. The exercise was to whittle those final five words down to one which would represent my "word of the year".

I struggled and stumbled over each choice, frustrated by the limits that were being placed on me.

Why only one? They're all important, aren't they?

It was afterwards I realised the importance of the word I chose.

That word was Courage.

And I did need it. He passed away in June 2018.

It was a tough time that required courage at so many stages and in so many decisions.

The following year I chose Joy.

What better antidote to grief.

What better tribute to my dad.

My dad only ever wanted joy for me.

So when you choose the values for your business; those 5 words that your business will live by or even your word of the year, resist the temptation to yawn at yet another values exercise. Do it so it matters. Do it so it counts.

When it counts, you'll be "all in" on this journey and another step closer to reaching your potential.

They will make decision making easier because you'll look to them for guidance.

They will make you happier because your work will be fully aligned with who you are as a human.

They are a tangible ingredient to what success means for you.

Reality Check. This Takes Work

It's tough, isn't it? This inner work that makes you choose yourself at long last. The realisation that you have to be vulnerable enough to show yourself how brave you are.

To let go of the mask that you are happy with the status quo.

A declaration to the world that you want something more and are prepared to do what it takes to get it. But this is not about hustle. It's not a test of how far you will go to get what you want.

It's an honest question that you must answer for yourself.

What is the work that you are willing to put into this worthy endeavour?

And what are the boundaries you will put in place to protect yourself?

This is important. Your next leap in your business is not meant to break you.

Your next leap needs to be designed to free you.

Your next leap

is not meant to break you

Design it

to free you

So, at each key decision point, remember to take a pause and tune in.

Tune into moments that are flags that indicate a closer look as opposed to assuming you're simply operating outside your comfort zone.

Sometimes you're nervous because you are right to be nervous.

Something isn't in alignment with what you are doing.

Sometimes you are nervous because you're reaching for the stars.

Start to hone your ability to tell the difference.

Alignment is a real clue here.

Does it make sense based on the destination?

Does it make sense in terms of leveraging everything you've worked for so far?

Every expansion is not the right expansion for you.

The clever leap is in choosing the one that fits.

This is where we find ease in our own growth.

Hear the Whisper

Thank you for hearing me at long last. That voice that whispered to remind you of who you are and that more is possible. I'm so proud that you chose to stand up for what you believe in.

I'm so proud that you chose to stand up for me.

Because I am the YOU you were meant to be.

And I am proud of you.

ENDNOTES

1. Box Breathing App by Unbeatable Mind is very useful here.
2. My "ex" that I mentioned at the start of this book.

SECTION 2

STOP DEFLECTING AND OWN YOUR BRILLIANCE

Here's where I draw attention to the times when you are in your zone of genius.[1] The times when you are fully engaged, do your best work and when you are at your happiest. I want you to remember those times now. They are unique to you and your work and only you can know them.

It could be a moment when you've captured a conversation inspiring those who listened with words that freed them in some way, written a piece of code that connected every other line of the program so it made sense, produced a work of art that fills the soul, created a formula for a product that would change how someone lived their lives, recorded a meditation that gave peace to someone who was troubled, coloured someone's hair so they walked with confidence in their own beauty.

The possibilities for genius are endless. The possibilities for your genius are known only to you.

When you are in those moments, you don't hear the doubts or feel the limits. This is where you glimpse your own brilliance. You feel the flow[2] at your core and you know you're there.

Sometimes you doubt the truth of it, so you quickly seek approval from those around you. You're hoping they will take you back to that moment of brilliance again. To confirm what you suspect is your life's calling. And when they do, it feels hollow in comparison. You don't quite believe it. If anything, seeking their approval diminishes the sense of brilliance you glimpse. So you retreat back to the everyday again.

But you've had enough of the everyday. You want to tap into that feeling of flow all the time now. And not just when you deliver your work. You want to feel it in all your life and you want to know how.

This is what I want you to remember. When you truly embrace the fullness of who you are, you won't need anyone else's approval. The only permission you need is already yours to give. And once you've given yourself that permission a whole new world will open up to you. You will take action that embodies this new belief in yourself and you will finally walk the path you choose.

ENDNOTES

1. Hendricks, G, *The Big Leap: Conquer Your Hidden Fear and Take Life to the Next Level*, HarperOne, 2010.
2. Csikszentmihalyi, M, *Flow: The Psychology of Optimal Experience*, Harper Perennial Modern Classics, 2008

4: THE ONLY PERMISSION YOU NEED IS ALREADY YOURS TO GIVE

You're starting to believe now; to believe that the real you doesn't have limits. And yet there seems to be two conflicting ideas from old conditioning running around in your head. You hear them – "be your best" but not "too much".

That "too much" is often expressed in several different ways. You might find a couple of these familiar:

- Be quiet, you're too loud.
- You've a big presence. That's very intimidating for people. You need to dial it back.
- I'm not showing you what's next. You'll have to wait until everyone else catches up.
- Stop being so successful. It makes us all look bad.
- You think too much.
- You're too sensitive, too soft, too open...
- You're too creative, too colourful, too different and so on.

And my personal favourite: "your signature is too flourishy", and "you're wearing too much red" which I was told in one of my annual reviews when I worked for KPMG.

TOO

MUCH

RED

When you share your "too much" stories out loud, you'll realise how many others have these stories too. You'll also realise how ridiculous it is when you say it out loud. It simply makes no sense.

Get the "Too Muchness" Log of Ridiculousness at <u>www.toldandshared.com</u>

Your "too muchness" is a beautiful signpost to your inherent uniqueness.

Your "too muchness" is your light shining brightly.

Follow that light.

Be grateful for what it shows you.

Prioritise Yourself First

I'll bet you're gasping in horror at this section title.

The tug in your stomach that makes you feel like you "shouldn't".

Your children, your family, your obligations; they all should come first, shouldn't they?

If I put my self first, that means I'm a bad person.

But this is not about everyone else.

This is about making a shift in your thinking so you stop waiting for it to be your turn and you start creating space for it to happen. Deliberate, intentional, unequivocal space for your dreams to breathe and unfold.

This is about giving yourself permission for more, much more. Your success does not have to wait for its turn in the mix of life's responsibilities. It gets to be put on the table for discussion with everything else. In fact, it has to or else how can it become real?

Too often, the things we need to do to create our own success are not even given a voice in the list of life's priorities. There's an assumption that we can make space for it later when everything else is taken care of. But it's too late then. If you wait to make space for it later you may stop hearing its whisper.

Your success was never designed to be at the expense of anyone else's path. Nobody has to suffer for you to shine. In fact, the world suffers when you don't let yourself shine. What you do need is to give voice to it. To make space for it. And "What If" comes into play again.

What if we did it this way?

When you prioritise yourself first, you invite the people who matter to you, to join you on your journey. That gives them permission to take their own journey too. It opens a conversation where everyone can get creative and ask the question – "If we did it this way, could we all get what we want"? How can we help each other so nobody gets left behind?

To enter that conversation, you start by knowing what you want and voicing it to those who can help you create space to receive it. By doing that you invariably create space for them to receive what they want too. Kevin, Sean and I actively do this together. We learned it first when we were planning that big campervan trip around France. We each got to pick where we wanted to go and then we just figured out a route that made it happen. It has been a powerful learning for all of us and one we've gotten better at over time.

Silence never supports your reach for the stars.

You've got to use your voice. Use it. You're worth it.

We are all worth it.

Diary Your "What If" Scenario

In Chapter 2, you built yourself a **What If Canvas™** and you used it to create space to articulate your vision of success in the world and you realised that "What If" doesn't need permission. It is imagination made real and action waiting to happen.

It's time now to lean in a little more to your **What If Canvas™**. You're ready to add depth to those first expressions of possibility. Your brain naturally wants to do this. You've presented a possibility that you'd like to explore and your brain wants to break that down into actionable steps to make it real.

This is when we see a transformation from "What If" to "Why Not" and "Why Not" requires action.

Why Not requires adequate space in your diary

Every Why Not has a natural path to follow, a series of steps to make it happen. Everyone's steps are different but the approach is always the same. It starts with clarification.

Let's explore that first "What If" I used as an example in Chapter 2.

What if I could stand on a stage and hold them all in the palm of my hands?

Immediately your brain is asking

- What does that mean?
- Stand on a stage? You want to speak or sing or act on a stage?
- What do you mean hold them in the palm of your hands?
- You mean you want to be really good at this? The best even?
- Okay. Do you need to learn something here?
- Who's the best person you could learn from?
- How can you find out? Google It?
- What about Fred – he knows that guy over there that did it before.
- Is there a course you can do?
- What are you going to speak about? What song will you sing? Which play will you be in?
- Let's find out more...

This is how your brain works. Whatever you want from this life. It says okay.

> *Whether you think you can, or think you can't - you're right.*
>
> — Henry Ford

You're serious about transforming "What If" into "Why Not". You've got the confidence now to believe in your own possibilities. You're ready to make this happen.

Choose the "What If" that shines brightest for you, the one you highlighted the most. Then get another blank sheet of paper and break it down into definable steps. Those steps can be reflective, research based, drafting something, drawing something, even a coffee conversation with a contact to tease something out. Every step is valid once it's with purpose.

Put each step in the right order and date them. There's no room for ambiguity here.

Now put them in your diary. They can't enter your diary without a name and a due date. Specificity is a powerful ally here. If you are too generic with your diary entry, you're effectively leaving yourself off the hook.

Your specificity will give you breathing room. There's enough detail to take action and yet not be intimidated by the prospect of actually achieving your dream. Every step gives you the chance to get used to the idea. It's that new suit of clothes that you need to grow into.

Make sure your "Why Not" has a daily entry into your diary.

This is an act of power and that act of power needs your commitment.

You are stating clearly that you mean to give this idea its due attention and everything it needs to come to life.

That is something you must do daily.

Even if the action required is reflection.

Once the reflection is done, it'll be followed by another action.

Give yourself permission to do that.

Choose People You Trust To Bear Witness

Every culture and language has a way to say hello.

In Irish we say *Dia Dhuit* which means God be with you. And in the wonderful way that we Irish like to one-up ourselves the answer will invariably be *Dia is Muire Dhuit*, which means God and Mary be with you.

Interestingly, if the greeting starts with *Dia is Muire Dhuit* we'll always find a saint of some description to add on to keep the conversation moving. So, it's often; *Dia is Muire is Padraig Dhuit* which means God and Mary and St Patrick be with you. We Irish always have something more to say, but I also like to think of it as a message that we are never alone. There'll always be someone to walk with you.

The Zulu people have their own greeting. They say *Sawa Bona.*

It's deeper than hello.

It means: **We see you.**

It's always "we". There is no "I" because, like the Irish, they believe they are never alone. They bring their whole lineage with them.

The response to *Sawa Bona* is *Sikhona*.

It means: **Because you see me, I am here.**

It is a moment of stillness where one appreciates the other.

It is a moment of bearing witness. Of giving our attention to another without judgement.

It is a supporting role; one of powerfully upholding the other.

This is what I ask you to seek out next.

To seek out witnesses who understand what this means for you and who you trust implicitly.

They are here to lend you their belief for the times when your own might flag.

They are the people who you can be vulnerable with, who know how far you've come.

They have no agenda except a shared journey where they too seek their next stage of growth.

It's a dynamic that doesn't compete. That has nothing to do except hold space for each other.

They do not want your power. They want you to hold your own and use it for your purpose.

I urge you to choose these witnesses wisely.

They have the power to deflate or to expand.

If the relationship is not expansive then it is not for you.

I know the difference because I've experienced both.

Let go of the ones who deflate as fast as you can and nurture the ones who help you expand.

They are your *Sawa Bona* team. Your "I see you" team.

Sawa Bona

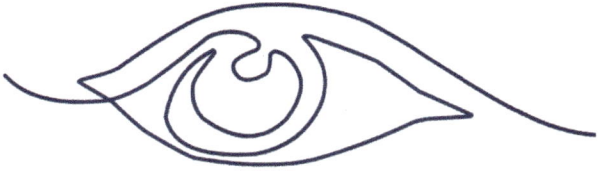

we see you

Be grateful for them. They will keep you on track.

I am ever grateful for mine. I'd like to introduce you to some of them.

I meet regularly with my accountability buddies, two powerful women; one in Ireland the other in the US. Our hearts are just forever connected. We took a mastermind together many years ago and we've borne witness to each others' journeys through many ups and downs. We are vulnerable and honest with each other. We are brave and grow independently of each other but still together. That is a powerful, powerful thing.

This book cohort that I'm part of, to write this book has already become a tribe of witnesses I value deeply. They show me the value I bring and push me when I don't speak to my own truth. I predict great things for this relationship as we continue our journey together getting our words out into the world.

The other group I cherish are the Mackerel Tassels who I sea swim with daily here in Dunmore East. They make me laugh, they push me to do things I've never done in the water before ☺ and they help me stand again when I fall. And did I say they make me laugh because yes indeed they do!

Closest to my heart are Kevin and Sean. They lend me their belief so much so that it's second nature now. It is simple, unequivocal and deeply appreciated. They show me that I could do this without them but I'll never have to.

This journey can be daunting but it does not have to be taken alone.

You know that your success will never be found in your silence.

You will need to share your story, your truth, your idea, your offering with the world.

Do it with those that value you first.

Hear the Whisper

I see you reader. I always did.

I'm so glad you're consciously creating a community around you that sees you too.

And because we see you, you are here.

Sawa Bona

5: YOUR ACTIONS WILL PROVE YOU WERE MEANT FOR MORE

Bravo you. You are still here reading. The layers of your own doubt are starting to fall away and it takes time to process them all and let them go. That is after all what we are doing here. Letting go of what no longer serves us.

Here's the one that often comes next. It can feel a bit odd to express, but I tell you: you are not alone in this one. It can seem irrational and yet you still haven't made peace with it.

Your clients tell you all the time the difference you make to them and you believe them. They write these powerful testimonials and you know on one level that they are true. But there's another part of you that feels like they're about someone else.

This type of dissociation is a defence mechanism against emotions that you find difficult to feel or make sense of. You might find it difficult to believe that the work you do is so powerful and impacts so many when you have not achieved the level of success (often financial) you expected at this point.

The culprit can be the often touted, nonsensical, limit-restricting, notion of "let the work speak for itself".

HOW CAN YOUR WORK SPEAK FOR ITSELF? IT DOESN'T HAVE A MOUTH!

Note my capitalisation here. Is that me shouting? Yes. Yes, it is.

This can also happen when you read back on past journals and the plans you made in the past but never actioned. Reading them can just feel like you're going around in circles and never getting anywhere.

They remind you of the recurring "What If" voice that you worry is getting quieter as time goes on. You want to believe that this time it will be different. This time you will finally believe you were meant for more and do something about it.

Belief Takes Action To Bring It To Life

You've reached a moment where you've got to decide, to put one foot in front of the other and just do it.[1] It is the look-in-the-mirror moment when the hero must face their doubts and fears and realise that, if they're going to achieve their goal, they'll have to step up and become someone new.

In Norse mythology, the ancient rune stones are often called upon for guidance in moments such as these. There is one rune stone that when pulled has nothing on its surface. It is the blank rune and is believed to be Odin's rune.

The blank rune is the end and the beginning. It portends a death: to a relationship, a way of life or a belief system. It is appropriate here.

"In each life there comes at least one moment, which, if recognized and seized, transforms the course of that life forever. Rely, therefore, on radical trust, even though the moment may call for you to leap empty-handed into the void."

– Ralph Blum[2]

I agree there comes a point on this journey where a degree of radical trust is required. The space between the known and the unknown; from where you are now to where you want to go does require that kind of trust. But it's never empty-handed. You bring everything you've learned with you.

You bring those testimonials, that buzz from those events you spoke at, and the times when you changed someone's life. Those moments when you know you made a difference. These are the facts that you bring with you.

It is the evidence of the difference you've already made in the world. It is the proof that you can show your inner critic to silence them. The facts speak for themselves. But that's not all.

You also bring those people you chose to bear witness for you. That's why we prepared the way with them in the last chapter. To shore you up so you can push through. So you can borrow their belief for a moment or two. Borrow it until you can do it for yourself and internalise the difference you are here to make.

Belief doesn't happen passively.

Build a path of small steps that will feed a new belief centred mindset. Start with steps that feel possible, that will take you to that next level.

They can be a commitment to write your book every day, to post on social every day, to send your emails every week to your mailing list, to finish that online course you are building, to launch that podcast, to figure out that ad campaign, or to hire someone for ten hours per month.

Commit to those steps. Show up for them every day and trust them.

Trust the small steps. They are your first tentative declaration of brilliance.

The more you do the more you will trust. The more you trust. The more you will believe.

Trust then do. Do then trust. Repeat.

Jennifer is a coach. She was finding it difficult to define how she was different to other coaches so she could grow her business. She joined my group program. As part of the process, we dug into her story; the evidence of her unique perspective. We suspected that one part was her ability to juggle life and business so successfully. There were others.

She tested each idea in her social posts to see which one would draw not only attention but discovery calls that converted. She was methodical and consistent, testing each one out and measuring the results. Her engagement grew exponentially as she found her voice, one post at a time. And as it became clear which messaging produced the best results, she did more of it. The more she did, the more her business grew.

Trust then do. Do then trust. Repeat.

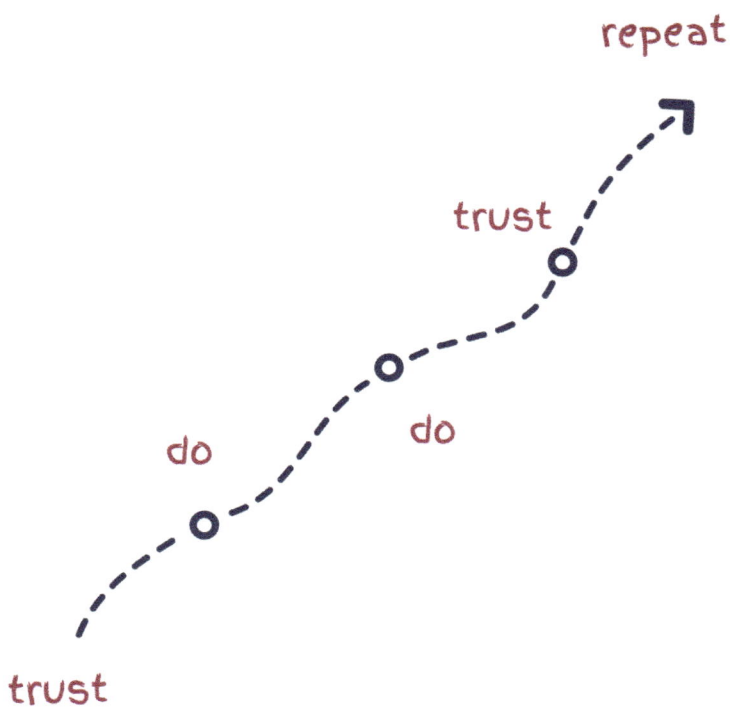

repeat

trust

do

do

trust

Know There's An Ebb And Flow To This Path

There won't be a single moment when everything happens for you all at once. It's incremental so you've got to pace yourself.

You have got to resist the temptation to "just work harder", to work later for "just one more evening" or forgo an occasion "just one more time". Because it's never for just one more time.

That hustle that everybody loves to speak about is actually a "serial killer" that's stalking you. It's killing those precious evenings, and important moments in your life again and again and again.

It gets pleasure from doing it. And it won't stop until you stop it.

I have played witness to too many stories of failed marriages, irrecoverable relationships with children, illness, burnout, fatigue and more. Too many stories like this from entrepreneurs who sacrificed in the name of success, to know it isn't worth it.

What is worth it is to be consistent. To take the journey at your pace. To help yourself believe more.

To invest in focus instead of effort. To spread the load.

And to remember, that you don't have to give it your all in every moment of every day.

This is about creating boundaries that make the journey worth it. Boundaries so you don't deplete yourself and give more than you should.

Little pockets of time that you give to yourself, to those you care about and to your business in a way that creates that flow and that success in this moment. In this moment here.

For yourself create pockets of time:

- To rest and sleep through the night a full eight hours.
- To break your fast, stretch as you get out of bed and nourish your body with food that sustains you.
- To take a moment and see the day as you would like it to go. Projecting what you commit to achieving and placing your focus there.
- To take a break in the middle of the day and have a meal enjoying it fully one bite at a time. Perhaps having a short walk in the fresh air, or a swim or cycle to reset and rejuvenate yourself.
- To stop at a reasonable time to enjoy each evening with your family, creating memories.
- To meditate and quiet your mind so you're not triggered by anything going on outside of yourself.
- To journal and reflect on the learnings of each day.
- To do what feels right for you.

For those you care about:

Create pockets of time to eat a meal together, to go to an event together, to hold one another, hear one another, have a chat together, laugh with each other and more.

You know best what you need to create space for. These are the moments we create memories in. They can't be rescheduled. They can't be postponed till later. Their time is now.

For your business:

Create pockets of time to focus on what matters.

I've said it already and I'll repeat it here.

Invest in focus instead of effort.

Choose where you'll place your attention and do that. Just that and only that.

It should be purpose driven and what you're best at.

When you focus on what you're best at, you get the best return.

When your best is spent on your purpose, you'll reach success much faster.

So, let every task that you place your attention on align with that goal.

If you find it hard to concentrate, get an app and use it to focus ten to fifteen minutes at a time. It'll stop you from getting distracted when you're doing tasks that don't require deep thinking, deep reflection or flow.

For bigger projects that do require that deeper level of concentration or flow, it's about breaking them down into bite sized chunks and taking consistent breaks to stay fresh.

When you break the bigger picture down, you can feel the progress as you go. In the case of my book I knew my target for every chapter was 2,222 words and 666 words in each section.

Those I could get my head around. Those kept me focused. Those I could make progress with. And then I could do it again.

Focus. Break. Focus. Break. Focus. Break.

Acknowledge each accomplishment, then celebrate with your *Sawa Bona* team.

They'll know what that progress means to you and help you anchor it for the next climb.

Expand Into Your True Power And Stay There

It's such a relief to realise that you don't need to seek approval or permission any more. It was already yours to give. To yourself.

Your belief in yourself is being bolstered with every action you take every single day. It is evidence of your commitment to yourself and the gift of your purpose. Know this: you are never given this gift without the power to achieve it.

As you expand into your power, your relationships may change with those around you. Sometimes that means the old power dynamics will have shifted, which can unsettle you and them. You are meeting the world as your truer self.

Get comfortable here. In this expanded version of you. There is more to come.

Centre yourself. Do not get swept away by ego. Instead start to understand the roles you play in your relationships, and how you can view them differently as you continue to expand.

In the 1950s, psychiatrist Eric Berne developed a form of psychotherapy called Transactional Analysis[3]. It looks at how we speak and respond to others and at the roles we play in our relationships. He identified three ego states or roles that everyone has: the Child, the Parent and the Adult. Each has their place in our lives at the appropriate time.

- **The Child State** is when we go back to feelings and actions that we would have engaged in when we were children. Our creativity, spontaneous actions and wonder come from here. So too do actions and feelings of sulking, brooding, pouting or sudden anger.

- **The Parent State** is where we often unconsciously imitate what our parents would have done in a situation. These can be things like criticising, scolding, advising, nurturing, encouraging and caring actions.

- **The Adult State** is the most objective of the three. It's stable, reasonable, and able to observe what is going on in the moment to make a rational decision.

It is useful to start to recognise the roles you play in each of your relationships as you expand. The goal is to improve those interactions so they become healthy and balanced. And if they can't be improved, perhaps they need to be let go of.

The goal of transactional analysis is to help people understand that each role has its place and purpose but that in most situations people should play the Adult role. Unless of course we're all jumping into the sea, being in the moment and having fun together.

Watch for this as you expand. You may find yourself playing the Child, the Parent or the Adult role in many relationships until you bring your attention to it.

Start to reshape those relationships until they all become Adult to Adult roles where both parties are leaning into this stable and reasonable approach to each other.

Remember this: your true power will never be found at the expense of anyone else. Nor will anyone else's true power be found at your expense.

I suggest these two rules to guide you:

- Any choice that makes you feel small is the wrong choice.
- Any choice that makes someone else feel small is the wrong choice.

There is another lesson here. Watch your own behaviour; where for whatever reason, conditioning or otherwise, you may unconsciously place your own power in someone else's hands. It's something I see when entrepreneurs are on the cusp of a next step move.

It can happen when they find a mentor or guide who is ahead of them on the journey and they are seeking to learn from them. Wherever they are on the journey, does not require that you become "less than" in order to learn. That's you disempowering yourself.

One of my greatest teachers in this was when I realised that the other person didn't want that responsibility. It was a subtle yet very powerful nudge. They had enough to be dealing with in their own lives. Their nonverbal "no thank you" was an urge to embrace my own power. I'll never forget it.

Hear the Whisper

I can hear the roots of your success taking hold. You are stronger now.

You will not sway in the wind when it comes to test you.

An ease is emerging as your inner power grows.

It is a confidence that I haven't seen before.

Embrace it. It is time.

ENDNOTES

1. Hat tip to Nike here for those powerful three words.
2. Blum, R, *The Book of Runes*, Angus & Robertson, 1990
3. Berne, E, *Transactional Analysis in Psychotherapy*, Souvenir Press, 1996.

6: IT IS TIME TO WALK THE PATH YOU CHOOSE

I remember getting to this point in my own journey. It felt like I was walking taller. In fact, I think I was. I stood straighter, felt lighter and could move with greater ease. There was nothing to weigh me down any more. The baggage I'd been holding on to for so long had just been laid down.

It feels easier, doesn't it when you realise that all that weight is in the past? You are grateful for what you learned and now you've let it go. Take with you the wisdom you earned and move forward.

And as you do, you will find yourself reaching for bigger projects that will increase your reach, your impact and your revenue significantly, and you can feel that expansion is possible. And then it hits you.

This new you, needs more than you've given before.

The old overwhelm tries to sneak in with cautionary tales of burnout, time constraints and so much to do. And this time you don't fall for it.

Welcome to the next level of you.

You know you don't need to panic. Progress has been made. Significant progress.

We're just going to keep going now. You've already started to fill the shoes of the new you.

Now it's time to go the rest of the way and fully occupy your truest self.

The Price Of The New Life Is The Old One

This is, perhaps, where a perceived sacrifice needs to be made. Where you must let go of that which no longer serves. You've chosen where you want to be, so now you need to spend your time on actions and thinking that serve that greater destination.

This is true expansiveness. To expand beyond yourself. When you choose to work only on that which delivers your next great leap and you need to build a team around you to support that leap.

It is the thing that scares so many entrepreneurs at this stage. To be responsible for someone else's income. To become a leader in your business. To set direction, to guide, to empower and to inspire others to help you. To draw people to you that are aligned with your values and who create ease in your business.

Too often, as entrepreneurs seek to grow beyond themselves, they get stuck here.

But you have grown. You know how to manage yourself now. You have clarity and focus. You can in fact, expand that clarity and focus to include others. But let's start with you.

"To know thyself is the beginning of wisdom."

– Socrates

With your "What If" focus and vision for what your success looks like for the business ask yourself what is your role in that success. Your clue is in what Dan Sullivan[1] calls your "Unique Ability" – a special talent that always has these four qualities:

1. **Superior skill**. You produce outstanding results with this talent. It's so natural to you, you can't help but do this extraordinarily well. Others notice this skill, rely on it and really value it.

2. **Passion.** You love to do this, and probably did it in some form long before you got paid for it.

3. **Energy.** Using your unique ability gives you a boost of energy. The people around you get energy from you too because it's fun and exciting to be around someone who's both passionate about and talented at what they're doing.

4. **Never ending improvement.** You're already exceptional at this, yet you could do it for the rest of your life and always find new ways to do it better and better.

As you start to recognise your own special talent ask yourself; what is the unique ability that you have that you could invest in and strengthen and do nothing else except that?

Then write your own future job spec where you use only that unique ability in the business. This is all you are being hired for. Nothing more. You will have heard of the 80/20 pareto principle which states that for many outcomes, roughly 80% of consequences come from 20% of causes. You are already familiar with it's application to business development which is the idea that 80% of your sales are coming from 20% of your customers.

So here's another "What If" for you.

What if 80% of your growth was coming from the 20% you are currently spending on your unique ability. And what if you spent 80% or 100% of your time and effort on your unique ability, what kind of growth could you expect then?

It's time to build on that, to invest in that. This is your next move.

Ask yourself; what will take your unique ability to the next level? What can you learn to make your unique ability even more powerful? This is your opportunity to move away from that stifling entrepreneurial necessity of having to wear so many hats in the business.

This is the gift of your next level growth. The gift of wearing just one hat. Your Unique Ability Hat.

Just One Hat

I always loved
the 1920s

You will be able to nurture the thing that you love to do and become even better at it.

Imagine the "What If's" that are clambering for your attention now.

Success Is Not Just A Head Game That Involves Only You

When you realise the possibility that you could craft a business that supports you at your best, doing what you love best, reaching further and higher, closer to your dream than you've ever been before, something shifts.

You realise that the freedom of entrepreneurship is achieved collaboratively.

And as you nurture to expand your own unique ability you also realise that you will need to build a unique ability team around you that does the same.

They will each be hired or contracted for the unique ability that they bring; that they too can nurture as you each play your part in the business.

With this perspective in mind, see what other roles are needed to support you to grow your business to that clear vision point you articulated in your What If Canvas™.

*"Growing does not mean hiring more **of** you.
Growing means hiring more **than** you."*

– Finola Howard

Growing means letting go of who you were to become the you you were meant to be. You will need this change of perspective at key points in your growth as you go from solopreneur to small business and beyond.

This letting go is not just a one-time thing. Be prepared for that. You will face it more than once.

Let me share with you three stories; two where these insights could have made all the difference to the businesses involved and one where it was truly embraced and the business flourished as a result.

A story for you as a solopreneur

Meet Chris. He just hired his first employee. This is the story he shared with me. "*I know he's not going to help me grow the business, Finola. I hired him to just to help me get some stuff done. I don't want him to be a challenge to me in any way.*"

I had that conversation about twenty years ago. The business is still the same size today. There was no space created for growth. That's the business that Chris wanted. It's the business he still has.

A story for you as a business with a small team

Over ten years ago, I had grown my agency business to a team of seven. I had read Michael E Gerber's *The Emyth Revisited: Why Small Businesses Don't Work and What to Do About It*. I knew I had to write the manual for new hires and create processes to support them so I did. I had invested in leadership programmes so that I could learn how to nurture my team and inspire them to follow a career path I had laid out for them.

But I hadn't laid one out for myself. I hadn't understood that I had to let go of who I was to nurture and invest in my own unique abilities. I carried the responsibilities of the whole business never leaving space for my own growth and in doing so I didn't build a "unique ability" team. I tried to recreate myself.

It's a common mistake and I did what every entrepreneur fears. I worked harder, for longer, sacrificing family time, time for my own wellbeing and more. It took me a while to figure out the lesson here. I dug deeper into the difference between leadership and management. I had always understood that leadership was about looking into the future, empowering and inspiring, and that management was about focus and execution of the plan.

I had both in place. I understood that I had a leadership role and I had hired a manager. What I came to appreciate was that I hadn't resourced myself first. I hadn't nurtured my own unique abilities and built the team around that.

Instead, the relationships, to be frank, were Parent/Child relationships if we go back to Transactional Analysis theory. This is a common trap, which I see more in women than in men. I recognise it immediately because I lived it.

It resulted in reaching a point where I chose to close the business. It was heart-wrenching, identity-wrecking and truly difficult.

But the business simply wasn't worth it as it was constructed then.

It was literally killing me. And closing it was the best decision I have ever made.

I put everything in order for the liquidator, handing over an identity that I truly believed in and had to let go of. I got clear guidance from him of what was allowable in terms of work so I could start again and generate an income for myself.

I will never forget the kindness of so many fellow entrepreneurs that rallied around me and supported me in my decision to start again the next day.

To not hide away as so many entrepreneurs do when this happens. To not succumb to the perceived shame associated with failure.

"A business may fail. A person learns.
They are not the same thing."

– Finola Howard

A business may fail. A person learns.

They are not the same thing.

Finola Howard

Today, I have a team of four. There is clarity in each of our roles and there is greater ease. I do the work that brings me joy. I swim every day. I meditate. I journal. I laugh. I spend time with family. I am happy.

I continue to invest in my own unique ability. You can see it in my courses, when I speak, in my podcast and in this book. And as I grow this unique ability my team will grow. It is my unique ability team where everybody has a clear role in the success of the business. More is coming. I'm excited by it.

A story for you as a business with a larger team

I once worked with a small business with about ten employees. There were two partners in the business who shared the role of CEO jointly, but it was keeping them stuck. It was appropriate as the business started, but as the business grew it simply became a bottleneck for growth. They had stayed at the same size and turnover level for about ten years.

This bottleneck became very clear in our work together. So, we focused on each partner's "unique ability" and how these abilities could be nurtured and strengthened. They both had to let go of some aspect of themselves and instead invest in their unique abilities. As a result, their roles changed fundamentally. One partner became the sole CEO and the other became the CTO. Both invested in themselves in these roles unhindered by the constraints of the old versions of themselves. The result? They doubled their turnover in three and a half years, a year and a half ahead of schedule, developed a new technology product which positioned them uniquely in the market and they are going from strength to strength with over forty-six employees today.

> *"If you know how to hire the right team members, you can build a Unique Ability Team that will allow you to expand your capabilities and exponentially grow your business."*
>
> – Dan Sullivan

The lessons are clear. Start with your unique ability and your vision for the business. Build from there. It will allow you to think much more expansively about yourself first and then the unique ability team that you build around you.

Your team may include freelancers, contractors, advisors or employees. They each have a clear role to play. And so do you.

You will change. You will change in a way that brings you joy. You will grow.

You will grow because you understand that you must let go of that which no longer serves you so you can create space for more.

Receive The Gift That You Are Here With Purpose

Can you see your focus already shifting? You have accomplished two key things here.

- Firstly, you have shed yourself of all the history and conditioning that weighed you down and prevented you from moving forward.

- Secondly, you have embraced the expanded version of you. You are seeing your own unique ability with fresh eyes, and are committed to nurturing that ability in yourself and in your growing team. In doing so you will nurture the uniqueness of your business and set it up for success.

This unique ability is yet another reminder that you are here with purpose. Both are so intertwined that it will become even more undeniable now in this new expanded version of yourself.

I invite you to revisit your What If Canvas™ with these fresh eyes. I bet it looks small in comparison to what is possible now. What would you write now? Would you change anything? Would you dream bigger?

Does the difference you are here to make in the world feel clearer, more possible, and more actionable? Are you now able to receive the gift that you are here with purpose.

That it is not a responsibility to weigh you down but an adventure you are excited to have?

There is a knowing attached to this gift that is expansive by its very nature.

Trust it. Trust that this is where you are meant to be. Trust that you are supported by everything you need to achieve it.

This is something to be grateful for. Keeping a gratitude journal is a powerful daily practice that allows us to appreciate the success we already have in our lives.

It is proven to have a positive impact on our mental attitude.

When you write in your gratitude journal now, start to include the strides you have made towards achieving your purpose.

It will allow you to receive it more fully and add a forward momentum to your thinking as you embark on this next stage of your adventure.

Your purpose is something to be grateful for and to be reciprocated with action.

Hear the Whisper

Thank you, for hearing me at long last.

The truth is, that whisper you've been hearing all along has been your own voice.

You've realised that now haven't you?

And it's getting louder with every page you turn.

Don't stop here. Keep going.

We're on an adventure after all.

And this is an adventure worth having.

ENDNOTES

1.   Sullivan, D and Hardy, B, *10X is easier than 2X: How World Class Entrepreneurs Achieve More by Doing Less*, Hay House Business, 2023

SECTION 3

TRY THESE NEW TRUTHS FOR SIZE

When my son Sean was little, everyone would ask "Who's he like?" My friends and family liked to say, "He's like you, Finola," and Kevin's friends and family liked to say, "You didn't get a look in, Finola, he's like Kevin!" And my lovely wise and diplomatic Dad always said, "He's like himself."

It is as true then as it is today. And that's what you are starting to realise too. You are like yourself.

I remember the moment when I looked in the mirror and realised something so simple yet so powerful. I realised what I'm good at. I'm good at being me.

It's the only thing I've ever been good at and it's the only thing I ever need to be good at.

So do that for yourself. Give yourself that breakthrough moment. Embrace the idea that the only thing you ever need to be good at is being you. The "real you". We talked about it in Chapter 3, and how you could use joy as the compass that takes you to that real you. That's when everything falls into place and expands.

And your view of what is possible expands without the weight of all those blocks that stopped you from seeing a way through before. There will be things you realise you don't know, but they won't scare you.

It won't matter that you haven't been here before. It won't matter that you don't have anyone in your circle that has been at this stage, yet. It won't matter because your world has just opened up, and as you embrace this next level of you, you know that this will all fall into place.

You will nurture this expansion by staying centred in this new relationship with yourself so you can deepen and expand what you are here to do.

So let's challenge the old rules for how we navigate our own path to next level success. Let's rewrite them as the new truths that make sure this is indeed an adventure worth having.

7: YOUR JOY IS A COMMERCIAL DECISION

Joy is never discussed in business circles. Happiness is. A little.

Happy customers, happy suppliers, happy employees, happy investors etc. When everyone is happy, the business succeeds. But happiness is fleeting. It is there in a moment and can be gone in the next. Joy, on the other hand, is a more long lasting state of being. Knowing the difference can change your perspective and your approach to life and business success.

Commercial success describes a business's ability to generate profit using its resources. In other words, a business with commercial success is one that is making enough money to continue operating, innovating and growing.[1]

If you dig a little more you'll come across the usual ingredients of good leadership, creating a business plan and sticking to it, obtaining and retaining customers, effective sales processes, creativity, strategic focus, effective systems, marketing, finance etc.

I don't contest any of these. They are all true.

The thing is, in my 30+ years in marketing and business growth, most of my time is spent on the things we've been exploring in the last few chapters. The greatest leaps are made firstly when we remove friction and secondly when we introduce joy and purpose. When the friction is gone, both joy and growth move in.

Let's introduce the notion then, that your business needs to be joyful to truly succeed. That your joy in what you do can be your true compass for sustainable growth. That it is a tangible indication of what you are best at and what your unique ability is. An indication that you, your team and your business are maximising your zones of genius.[1]

"Joy is not a 'someday' phenomenon in your life or in your business. It's a success imperative."

– Finola Howard

One of the things that has always frustrated me when people speak about what it takes to succeed is the assumption that "joy" is a "nice to have". That's simply not logical. Logic dictates that "the simplest solution is almost always the best." – Occam's Razor[2].

I remember several years ago, on one of my Get Strategic™ programmes, there was a business who wanted to make science more accessible to school kids by showing them that rocket science was, in fact, easy. It was a "go-to" statement of mine at the time that I subsequently had to rethink. So, we all laughed any time I found myself falling into the trap of saying "it's not rocket science" when demystifying some marketing technique.

And just so you know, there are, in fact, only three basic requirements to a working rocket and **I've included plans to make your own rocket here at <ins>www.toldandshared.com</ins> just to prove the point.**

If we apply Occam's Razor to what we will call the "success conundrum" then Joy has to play a pivotal role. It yields the greatest clarity that you are in the right place, doing the right things with and for the right people.

Joy Facilitates Growth In The Right Direction

Joy doesn't let you get bored or stuck in a rut. Joy stops when you enter the comfort zone. It sings when you are in your zone of genius. It's the indicator of when it's time to move to your next level and it's the armour that stops you from being afraid of growing.

Your joy is personal to you.

Where you do your best work is not where I do mine.

And that means we each need a different compass for our own growth. My compass is not your compass. The greatest success stories have always built their own compass.

Their own view of the world and how they wanted to make it better.

"Here's to the crazy ones, the misfits, the rebels, the troublemakers, the round pegs in the square holes... the ones who see things differently — they're not fond of rules... You can quote them, disagree with them, glorify or vilify them, but the only thing you can't do is ignore them because they change things... they push the human race forward, and while some may see them as the crazy ones, we see genius, because the ones who are crazy enough to think that they can change the world, are the ones who do."

– Steve Jobs, 1997

If you are reading this book, you are one of the crazy ones. You are the Einstein, the Muhammad Ali, the Earhart in your space. Imagine that. Imagine if you could give yourself permission to be good enough to be you, like they did. Imagine what you would accomplish.

Start by building your "Joy / Release Compass™"

The Joy / Release Compass™ is a transformational model for next level growth that I've developed that you will use to ensure you consistently move towards your own next level success; one characterised by joy, fulfilment, freedom, abundance and all the other things you want for yourself.

It means you will have left behind the meandering, roller coaster ride that typifies the entrepreneurial journey. You will have found ease in your own growth and because there is ease, you are no longer afraid of it. And when you are no longer afraid, you will have found ease in your own connection to yourself.

There was a time in my life where I fought against ease, where I thought growth had to be hard. It's that old conditioning that you had to work hard for anything truly important.

And then I met a lady who bothered me. It was on one of my adventures in Sedona, Arizona.

There was I, agonising over my own personal growth, railing against it all, pushing through that caterpillar-like stage, breaking through. It was just so hard; breaking free of my old cocoon.

And there she was: smiling. And it just kept niggling at me. I assumed she just wasn't doing the work. So, in the end, I asked her.

And she turned to me and smiled again and said, "I just set the intent, Finola, that there would be ease in my growth here." Amazed, I asked, "Can you actually do that?"

And she replied, "Why not? Who said it had to be hard?"

flying is easier

when you soar

Mind blown. I thanked her and walked away. I try to remember that lesson as much as I can. And when I do. The growth does, in fact, come with ease.

Know this. It's not that it's easy. It's that you can choose for it to come with ease. Ease comes with mindset and preparation. Ease comes with joy. Both are fundamental to your compass.

The Joy / Release Compass™
for Sustainable Business Growth

Your compass is a simple arrow pointing towards joy.

It is characterised by movement. Movement ahead towards joy and a release of that which no longer serves behind, with a centre that indicates a journey inward to find the stillness that creates ease.

When you are growing, your compass is constantly moving because it's the flow that matters. Your compass is designed to clear any obstacles to that flow. This is why the base of the compass is about release. It's about letting go of anything that is not joyful and therefore not in your zone of genius so you can continually create space as you move forward.

Feel the movement as you imagine yourself holding it in the palm of your hand.

Feel also that when everything you do is in alignment, you not only expand but move faster too.

Purpose is what guides you towards Joy

It's what will push you forward. You've accepted the gift of your purpose. You've realised that you belong to your purpose and your purpose belongs to you. This is how you move towards joy.

This is where opportunities open up, expansion occurs and momentum is achieved. It is the opening up before the release.

The centre of the compass is the pause point

This compass seems so simple and yet simple is often not easy. That's why you will seek ease in that centre point. It's where you will connect in with yourself again. Over the Temple of Apollo at Delphi is the inscription "Know Thyself", and that is what is characterised in this part of your compass.

This is where you will pause when you don't yet know what to do, so anything you do will be out of alignment with who you are. Trust this centre space because it's where you will hear the whispers of yourself again to guide you.

The pause point is your most creative space. It is where transformation occurs. Remind yourself: just because you're changing doesn't mean your business is broken. It means you are creating space for flow again. You are innovating. You are growing.

In Norse Mythology, the rune for the "self" is joy and its mirror image, and it teaches that rectification comes before progress where the self is fully aligned to the self. From this place everything becomes clear. So we create space for alignment with who you are and what brings you joy here in the pause point.

"Go into your cell and your cell will teach you everything there is to know. Your cell. Yourself."

– Abba Isidore,
Monk from the 4th and 5th Centuries

The Self

and it's mirror image

Remember that, even more than we are doers, we are deciders. Once the decision is clear, the doing becomes effortless.[3] Allow yourself to rest here. To decide. To pause when you need to. To know that in this pause you are still pursuing joy. In fact, the deepest part of your transformation is happening here in this space.

If you feel you are stationary too long, let go of something to nurture the flow again. Remember that even in the pause point movement needs to happen. Your reflection here is creating space to allow those things to happen. If that reflection turns into a repeating pattern, it's no longer reflection. It is a block to your own growth.

The base of your compass is about release or delegation.

This is perhaps the most courageous part of your journey. It is the point where you let go of "should" and expectations so that you can move forward into the unknown. This is where you let go of the work that no longer brings you joy. It's where you choose what no longer fits you or your business growth.

If it's something that the business requires in order to grow, then it's something worthy of delegation. Let's be clear here: delegation does not mean abandonment. Delegation is a balancing act of systems, education and release.

You are clear on what needs to be done and that the best person to do it is no longer you. Don't hold on too tightly to what brought you here. Do be clear on how you define what needs to be delegated.

It's got to be ring fenceable, and easy to see that it contributes to growth tangibly. And then you've got to release it into the safe hands of the right people for this role.

Your Joy / Release Compass™ is practical and grows with you

The things that bring you joy will change and grow with you. The things that drove you forward toward purpose before may now represent a need to release or to delegate.

Allow them to move. Don't attach yourself to them. See them for what they are. The powerful memories of your own personal growth.

Pay attention to four key areas with your compass

1. **Purpose Clues** which are signposts to your uniqueness, which, when viewed together, point to the next level of you. Note them in the purpose areas of the compass.

2. **Purposeful Outcomes** are that next level of you in your business. They can be an initiative in your business or the direction of the business itself. Note them at the tip of your compass. These are destination points along your journey.

3. **Pause Points** are the insights you gain when you bring clues and outcomes together. They may also indicate future clues as you find yourself articulating and reflecting on them. Note them in the centre of the compass.

4. As you grow, those once powerful purpose clues evolve into **release points**. Areas of the business where you are no longer the best person to deliver on them. Release points are where you choose to let go or delegate something in the business. Note them in the base area of the compass.

Let me share with you some practical lived examples and how they apply to the compass.

Example One – Your Truth Shared Podcast with Finola Howard

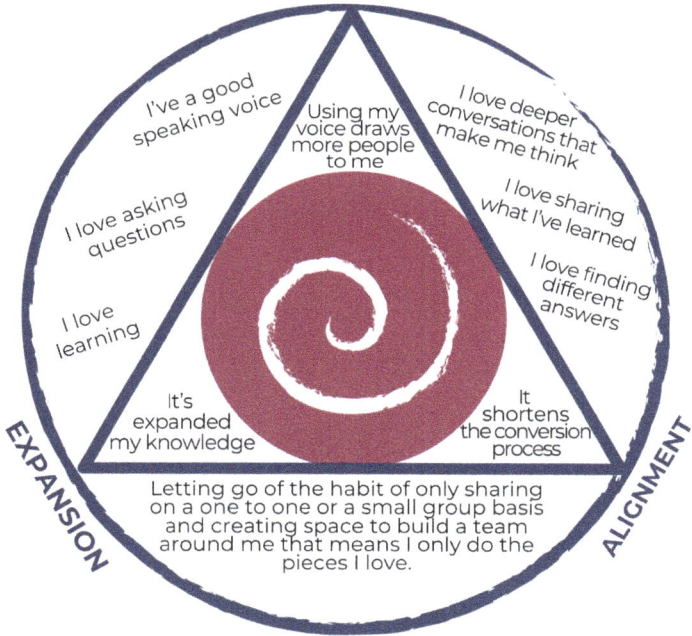

Your Truth
Shared Podcast

I've a good speaking voice

Using my voice draws more people to me

I love deeper conversations that make me think

I love sharing what I've learned

I love asking questions

I love finding different answers

I love learning

It's expanded my knowledge

It shortens the conversion process

Letting go of the habit of only sharing on a one to one or a small group basis and creating space to build a team around me that means I only do the pieces I love.

EXPANSION

ALIGNMENT

1. **Purpose Clues** I've a good speaking voice, I love asking questions, I love deeper conversations that help me think differently or find different answers, I love expanding my knowledge, I love sharing what I've learned with my clients in order to help them on their journey.

2. **Purposeful Outcome** – Your Truth Shared Podcast

3. **Pause Point** Using my voice has drawn more people to my work on a global scale. It's shortened the conversion process and expanded my knowledge.

4. **Release Point** Letting go of the habit of only sharing on a one to one or a small group basis and creating space to build a team around me that means I only do the pieces I love.

Example Two – Rosemary Daynes Kearney - See Podcast Episode #82 How Self Love can Turn Our Darkest Moments into Opportunities.

A Purposeful Business that Speaks to Head & Heart

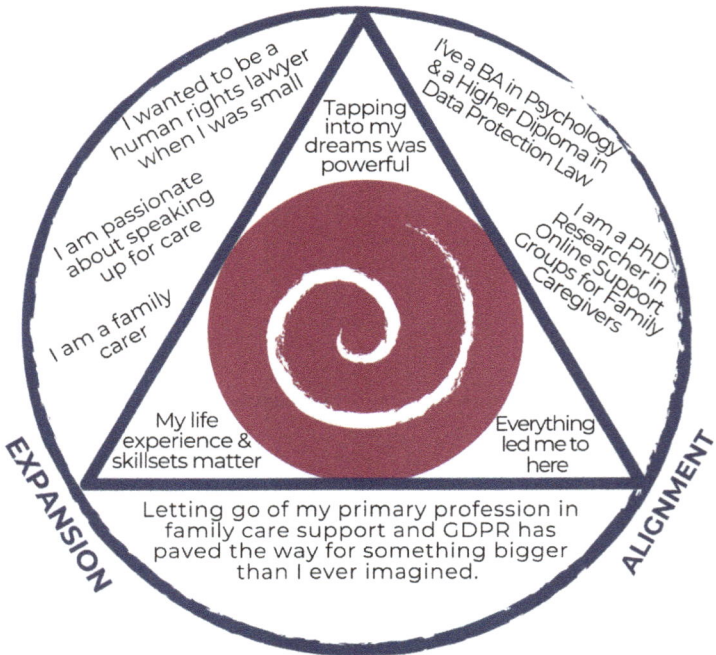

1. **Purpose Clues** I wanted to be a human rights lawyer when I was small, I am a family carer, I've a BA in Psychology and a Higher Diploma in Data Protection Law, I am passionate about speaking up for care, I am a PhD Researcher on the topic of Online Support Groups for Family Caregivers.

2. **Purposeful Outcome** – A Purposeful Business that Speaks to Head and Heart

3. **Pause Point** Tapping into my dreams as a young girl and my subsequent life experience and skillsets has shown me a way to make my real difference in the world.

4. **Release Point** Letting go of my primary profession in family care support and GDPR has paved the way for something bigger than I ever imagined.

Example Three – Amanda Webb - See Podcast Episode #79 Google Analytics Secrets that Will Propel Your Business

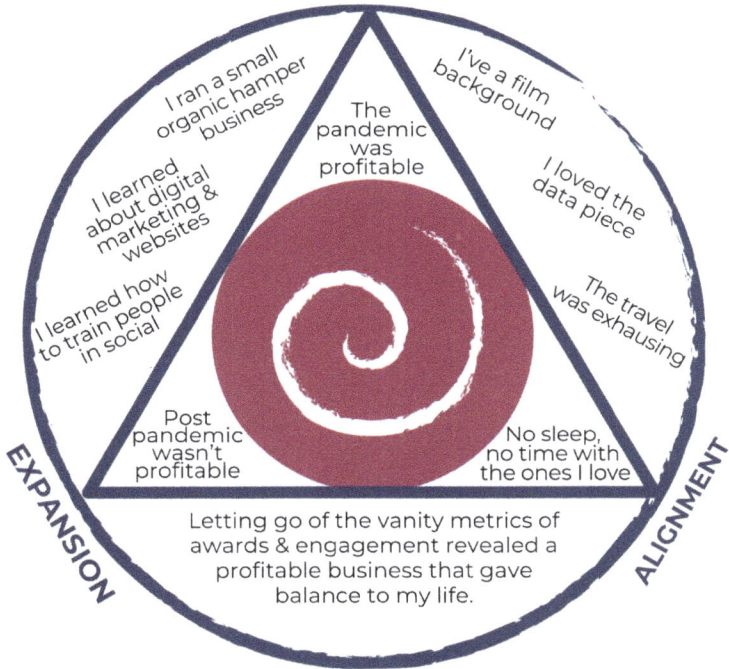

A Niche in ROI & Analytics

Text within diagram:
- I ran a small organic hamper business
- I learned about digital marketing & websites
- I learned how to train people in social
- The pandemic was profitable
- I've a film background
- I loved the data piece
- The travel was exhausing
- Post pandemic wasn't profitable
- No sleep, no time with the ones I love
- Letting go of the vanity metrics of awards & engagement revealed a profitable business that gave balance to my life.
- EXPANSION
- ALIGNMENT

1. **Purpose Clues** I ran a small organic hamper business, I've a film background, I had to learn about websites, social media and digital marketing to make the business work. I love data. The travel and in person training was exhausting and unprofitable.

2. **Purposeful Outcome** – A Niche in ROI and Analytics

3. **Pause Point** The Pandemic was profitable. The period after the pandemic wasn't. I didn't sleep enough or spend enough time with the ones I love.

4. **Release Point** Letting go of the vanity metrics of awards and engagement revealed a profitable business that gave balance to my life.

Using the Joy / Release Compass™ simplifies decision-making

You remain focused on tuning in to yourself and why you are here. Your decisions all lead towards purpose and let go of that which no longer serves you. You won't have to wear so many hats in your business anymore. You can let go of the ones that are not for you and pass them to someone who is excited to wear them instead.

You will have greater freedom in your life because your business doesn't have to be so all-consuming. You will have time for you, for rest, for play, for family, for friends, for community AND for your business.

This is not about balancing your life. It's about how you distribute the resources you have to bring you the greatest joy.

I've included the Joy / Release Compass™ with clear instructions on how to use it at **www.toldandshared.com** so you can get started on your own next level growth.

Joy Helps You Choose The Right People

It's always easier to hire when you hire for someone else. There are always established systems and processes that can guide you and it doesn't feel like there's so much at stake.

It's the biggest reason so many entrepreneurs don't grow beyond themselves. They feel the responsibility of someone else's livelihood and their part in that too deeply.

But when you hire well, you build your own path to freedom. You free yourself of the tasks that are no longer yours to do and now you know what they are. Your Joy / Release Compass™ is pointing you forward, and you're reflecting in that pause point.

You're getting ready to hire or outsource for the roles that allow you to let go and delegate. Take the time to make sure there is clarity in each role and it is capable of being self-managed.

Remember, they have a Joy / Release Compass™ too
The role you offer needs to be purposeful for them too. It needs to serve their joy. If it doesn't, there will always be friction and friction is an indication that joy is absent. Don't ignore it.

What you're looking for is the magic that happens when everyone is reaching for their purpose and that their purpose is aligned with yours.

Several years ago, I took a partner into the business. She was excited by what I was doing, and having a strong operational background she wanted to add that skill set to the business. It created space for me to do what I did best and grow the business.

Every day she'd hear me speak about doing what you love, tapping into the things that bring you joy, that help you achieve your purpose. Eventually, she realised that although she could do this role in the business, it's not what fired her up or made her happy.

So we parted ways and she went on to create a very successful, award-winning food service and catering company which she has just sold as she too moves on to the next stage of her growth.

Joy will always help you choose the right networks, the right staff, the right investors, the right customers. Joy will ensure you always choose people that are aligned with what you want to achieve.

Joy can challenge and support in equal measure and it'll be the same for them too. They'll know they are in the right place when they tune into their own joy (even if they don't realise it yet).

You'll know you have the right people with you, because they'll be smiling. If they're not smiling, they're not for you; whatever the role.

> *"When I was 5 years old, my mother always told me that happiness was the key to life. When I went to school, they asked me what I wanted to be when I grew up. I wrote down 'happy'. They told me I didn't understand the assignment, and I told them they didn't understand life."*
>
> – John Lennon

Establish Joy As A Key Success Metric

Joy is sustainable. There is an inherent flow and ease to it. It is where you do your best work. Joyful work is easier to pitch for, to deliver on and to build relationships with. You know this now.

The thing is, if you are truly serious about joy as an instrument for growth in your business, you've got to be able to measure it. Growth needs metrics.

You need to be able to benchmark how much joy is in your business, to change what's not working and measure again.

But what are the metrics for joy in a business
Is it the number of times you smile vs the number of times you don't. Well, it's a little of that. I found myself reflecting on all the times where I needed to make a shift in the business to bring back my own joy. They all revolved around five key things:

1. **Happiness of your customers.** Are they consistently happy with you?
2. **Happiness with your customers.** Have you chosen the right ones?
3. **Happiness with each service you provide.** Do you (still) like doing this type of work?
4. **Happiness on each project delivered.** Has every individual project made you happy?
5. **Happiness with each team member?** Do you like working with every member of your team?

If anything in these five areas didn't feel quite right, I always changed it. That change was always the right decision.

This is what I call the **Business Joy Scale™** and I've created a simple quiz so you can establish this metric in your business and check in on it regularly. Click here to take the quiz at www.toldandshared.com.

> *"Life's too short to waste your time doing things that don't light your fire".*
>
> – Richard Branson

As it becomes clear what lights you up and what doesn't, you'll find yourself letting go of the work, the customers and the team members that don't bring you joy. And life just gets a whole lot simpler. Go with it.

ENDNOTES

1. BBC Maestro Blog - https://www.bbcmaestro.com/blog/what-is-commercial-success
2. Occam's Razor is the problem-solving principle that recommends searching for explanations with the smallest possible set of elements or requires the fewest set of assumptions.
3. Blum, R, *The Book of Runes*, 1990, Angus & Robertson

8: MONEY IS A WORTHY MEASURE

When I've shared the title of this chapter, people have often thought I'd made a mistake. That what I really meant to say was that "joy is a worthy measure". But remember what we're doing here, we're challenging the old rules and rewriting them as the new truths that make sure this is indeed an adventure worth having.

You've already learned how to use joy as a tool that helps you tune into the right commercial course of action. Now let's use money as a tool to tune into what your heart truly desires.

Money is a very emotive thing in small to medium sized businesses. It's tied up in worth, in identity and even in purpose. I've had so many conversations and there's quite a few on my podcast where the business owner says "I'm not motivated by money". And I find myself constantly challenging the appropriateness of that statement.

But you've realised this already, haven't you?

You know how to make a living at your business. You always have "just enough" for what you need. You always "get by". You always "find it in the end".

But that's the thing. It's always "just enough".

You haven't made the level of wealth that you see on social media; with the yachts, the designer gear, that opulent lifestyle that seems to establish people as that next level entrepreneur.

And, in fact, that kind of lifestyle doesn't really interest you. What does interest you is Freedom.

What you need to decide is what that freedom looks like so you can figure out how much it costs and then reach out to get it. Is it the freedom...

- to write every day and pursue your love of sharing your knowledge,
- to take the time to look after a loved one in their final days (see episode #83 Scaling with Soul: the Human Side of Business with Marina Branigan),
- to travel the world and visit the places you've only ever read about in books while you're still young enough to enjoy it,
- to create something meaningful that has an impact on the world,
- to meet and work with your heroes,
- to leave a legacy, to make the way easier for those coming after you,
- to retire early, spend your winters in a warm country and summers in cooler climate,
- to sail that yacht around the world,

- to have time to be in the moment with the ones you love?

Like joy, your freedom and your next level wealth is personal to you. Only you can decide what that looks like. Let's explore how you can make that decision. It is your time to reach out for more.

Making A Difference Isn't Enough Any More

You've made a difference in so many people's lives with your work but your business needs to make a difference to your life too.

Money is a worthy measure because it's a **public declaration that you know you are worth it** and you've given yourself permission to show that you're worth it.

It's about taking power over your own choices against the conditioning you've had with money up until now. Many years ago, I signed up for a day long course run by a group called "Wealth of Women".

We started with a FREE (Fast, Raw, Exact but Easy) writing exercise for ten minutes. That means you have to keep the pen on the page, and keep writing until the bell sounds. It's a well-established technique to get you to access your subconscious. When you get stuck you might end up writing "This is crazy, I've nothing left to say here, what will I say, I know, what about that time when..." and so on.

And they gave us the prompt "Dear Money..." and we had to take it from there.

It was a powerful exercise. So cathartic. When we were invited to share what we had written, so many women had stories that brought them to tears, sharing their frustrations, their disappointments etc.

But the true learning happened with the second part of this exercise.

Our prompt this time was Dear (Insert Your First Name) and this time money was writing back to us.

So, so powerful what was unearthed. If you've never done this exercise, I highly recommend it.

Even better, do it with friends and share what comes. There is nothing more empowering than knowing you're not the only one.

Money is vital i.e. necessary for your vitality.

It's vital that you want some things for yourself too. We learned that wanting is deeply connected with growth. This is not greed or consumption for consumption's sake.

This is about defining your return on your investment.

What is it that you want for yourself?

What would make all this worth it?

Write down the answer to this question before you read any further. Do it quickly before you think too much about it. What kind of life, home, freedom, bank balance, retirement fund, college fund, car, clothes etc would make all this worth it?

How much would make all this worth it?

Doing The Numbers Will Empower You With Possibility

Have you done it? Have you written a number down? Okay, I'll wait here. Stick it in the notes of your phone if you can't find a piece of paper. I want you to see what happens the minute you clearly articulate what you want.

Watch. Can you see it happening?

Your brain has just kicked in to see how it can help you deliver on that desire.

Entertain that notion now. Bed it in.

This is what you want. No limits. No ifs, ands or buts.

This is what you want.

The limits to having this are only ever set in your mind.

They start to disappear when you take a closer look and then take action.

Taking that closer look is a declaration that you want something enough to come out of hiding and explore what it means to get it. Make friends with spreadsheets.

With every dream you have for your business look at the numbers.

What do they reveal? How much is possible?

This is an expansion exercise that will give you freedom from your own limits.

The most common challenge that people come to me with is their marketing.

That comes in all shapes and sizes: brand, positioning, customers, product, digital etc.

But when we dig into it, it's about how to make money or how to make more money.

The marketing is simply the vehicle to make that happen.

And the numbers reveal everything.

They teach you about pricing, packaging, business modelling, hiring, return on investment, conversions, engagement, time, costs, profit and so much more.

It all revolves around the lens you look through, how often you look and what you're willing to take action on.

The list is endless of the people I've worked with who have been empowered by their own numbers:

- Mary, who realised that her business was saleable if she adjusted how she worked and what she worked on,

- Joe and Sheila, who hid their business's point of difference in 100 products instead of 10 niche products that would showcase their expertise and increase their bottom line,

- Terri who realised that €1m turnover was just as easy to achieve as €250K if she hired for the tasks she'd grown out of and could release,

- Jenny, who realised that if she packaged her work so it was easy to buy from her could exceed her financial targets half way through the year and that much more was possible because she had started to carve out a space for herself,

- Fred and Tom, who hadn't grown their business in ten years doubled it in three because we saw they needed to spread their risk away from one key customer.

If you'd like to know more about these stories, you can access their case studies here at www.toldandshared.com

In every case, part of our work together was to look at the "right numbers" and then act on them. When they did, the world opened up to them. And freedom wasn't far behind.

Money doesn't judge. It empowers. If you let it.

Build A Healthy Active Relationship With Money

When you hide from the money question, you are operating from a place of fear, and you cannot realise abundance from a place of fear.

Expand into money. Expand into your own wealth.

Do it practically AND emotionally. Diary it so you can't hide from it. Set a consistent time in your calendar where you create space to look at the numbers.

You need the consistent truth of your numbers to set you free.

Look at it as a daily practice that you love to do and are rewarded with the ability to manage your own financial growth in real time.

As a daily practice, keep a financial scorecard. It takes between five and fifteen minutes per day to see where you are in cash flow, in profitability and in growth prospects. It'll prompt action to keep everything flowing and prioritise what matters.

As a weekly practice, keep your financial records consistently up to date ready to be finalised with your accountant at the end of each month. Look at them each week. What are they telling you? What action do you need to take to leverage opportunities or reduce risk?

As a weekly emotional practice, make friends with money.

Start with the Dear Money exercise. Write a letter to money to get to the bottom of this "just enough" money block.

When you're finished, have a cup of coffee and start again. This time it's money writing back to you and it starts with Dear [your name].

What comes? How is this making you feel?

Work through this to relieve yourself of blocks and expand into your own abundance. Remember abundance means you're always worth it.

You need the head AND the heart, the money AND the joy to make this adventure worth having.

Please take 5 minutes to leave me a review, it helps other people to decide if they want to read the book, and I'll be eternally grateful. If you're reading on Kindle just scroll to the end of the book. If you're reading the paperback, please go to your favourite bookstore.

Remember, you can get the promised downloads at www.toldandshared.com or scan the QR code.

9: YOUR VOICE BECOMES YOU

Now you know there are no limits to your own possibilities. You have expanded your idea of what's possible with your What If Canvas™ and you have a Joy / Release Compass™ to keep you on track.

It reminds me of something my mum always said to us when we were little. I only now realise where it originated. Go you, Mum!

> *"Nothing is impossible to those who try!"*
>
> – Alexander the Great

She used to say this to us, so we wouldn't give up, so we'd keep pushing and realise what we could do and what we could have in our lives. It's something she embodies every day, even now as she battles her Parkinson's. She amazes the nurse practitioner in her check-ups as she staves off the progression of this disease which claimed my Dad. She actively seeks answers, the things that she can do that make a difference and she accepts her own capability in this journey. It is truly inspirational.

The next step for you on this adventure is to accept your capabilities, your brilliance with the ease you have now chosen for yourself. To allow yourself to celebrate YOU with your own voice.

To be excited and unencumbered. There is nothing to be afraid of here.

You are here because you are meant to be. You are here because you have work to do.

To do "your" good in the world and to be good to yourself.

Let yourself enjoy it. Be proud of how far you've come. And get ready for more.

Your People Are Waiting; Tell Them You're Here

Your voice is the keeper of your truth. It holds the power to your uniqueness and to your place in the world. When you use it, unencumbered by everything you've let go of here, you will step more deeply into yourself and your uniqueness will rest more easily on your shoulders.

I remember working with a client, some time ago, who wanted to leave her job and create the business that would feed her soul. She hadn't left her job yet. She hadn't quite stepped into this next iteration of herself.

She was still one foot in the job which was crushing her spirit and one foot in the business which would release her.

Her job was in the professional space and she held it with confidence and the certainty of her own abilities. You could tell this, by the sound of her voice and by the posts she would put out on social media.

Conversely, when she spoke about the business she wanted to create, the volume of her voice dropped often to a whisper, so much so she often didn't finish her sentences but left them to be completed by the listener. She didn't quite yet believe that her success in this space was truly possible, even though she was taking steps to make it so.

Our first piece of work together was to build a habit of finishing her sentences in a strong and certain voice, so that she could get used to the sound of her future self. So that her voice could become her.

At the same time as she worked through this habit building process, we looked at the numbers. We calculated what she needed to earn to leave the job and the other "wants" she articulated. We built out the revenue model and packaged her products and services so that they would be easy to sell.

It was all doable. Her voice paved the way and knowing the numbers empowered her.

She has since left her job and this new business of hers is thriving.

Sometimes your voice needs to go ahead of you

Not just any voice. Your true voice needs to pave the way and be heard. That unique perspective that you bring to the world. Your voice in all the ways you communicate: in sound, in video, in writing, in social media, in articles, in interviews etc.

Yes, it's about visibility, but not at any price.

It's about your message, your unique perspective, the reason you're here. In your words, with your tone and your truth.

And as you start to speak it, it will become stronger. And your people will respond.

If you dilute it with anything else, you'll dilute your impact and that will miss the point of all the work you've done here. Speak with authority, authenticity, and relatability.

Speak from your "What If" voice. Speak from your heart.

Speak to the "one" not to the many.

The "many" will follow when you focus on the "one".

The more you speak, the more confident you will become.

As you reach the "one", your voice will get louder and you will finally be heard.

Feel Your Voice Change From A Whisper To A Roar.

It is a beautiful, beautiful thing.

Create Your Own Stage And Fill It With Joy

You've left permission-seeking behind you.

You've come with a pure heart and a clear goal. You can't stop now.

Don't wait to be asked to be on someone's show, or to speak at someone's event.

Ask for your spot, show up, be seen, be heard.

Be seen and heard in the space you want to own, wherever your people are and in the media they consume. Be seen and heard for all you are in the new reflection you see in your mirror.

Take yourself to the next level.

And if you can't find a stage right now, create your own and make it yours.

Launch your own podcast, write your book or create your own event.

Do it your way. Doing it your way creates the space in the world that you know you were meant to take up. And you will draw others to you.

Formulas are great and we use them to speed up the process.

Just remember this, if everyone is using the same formula, you'll just blend in.

And you're done blending in.

Keep tuning in to you and your difference will shine.

Your voice will become you with every word you speak.

And this business that means so much will relax into itself as you realise you are in the right place.

You are here doing what you were meant to do, at long last.

And at the edge of this great adventure, you will see a glimmer of what's next.

And it's calling to you.

And this time your answer will be yes.

You're not afraid any more. You're just doing more of you.

That's all. And that's enough.

There is no need to lean in and listen for whispers any more.

You know your own voice when you hear it.

And you like how it sounds.

It's the sound of the choices you make freely that bring you joy.

There is no better sound.

What If We All Stopped Hiding?

For over twenty-five years, I've been holding space for the powerful voices that stay hidden. They are the entrepreneurs who care, the ones who spend their days making a difference but rarely take the next step for all the reasons I've been sharing in this book.

They are you and they are me. One of the key people I wrote this book for was me.

It has helped me ease into my own brilliance and release my own blocks in equal measure.

Some I had dealt with years ago and the others were the sticky remnants that hold on that little bit tighter until they could truly be released.

I have grown from writing this book. I am different because of it.

Ease was the final ingredient for me. The surrender that comes when you hear your own truth.

This is not the book I started to write. This is the book I needed to write.

I knew it needed to be written because I needed to read it.

I needed to be able to show the many entrepreneurs I've helped over the years how to break through this next barrier. I hope it did that for you.

So, in celebration of who you already are, I invite you to consider the notion of so many people like you and me in the world and imagine a future where we all stopped hiding. Where we all decide to be brave enough to choose the success that we define for ourselves and share our truth. Will you join me?

If that's a yes, please register and log your beautiful brilliance here at <u>www.toldandshared.com</u>. Post a video or a picture. Come out of hiding and share your truth. Share what you are here to do in the world and the unique perspective you bring.

And if you're feeling really brave. Share it on social media. Tag it with #Thisismypurpose #MyTruthShared.

Pave the way so others can find their ease faster.

So we can all make our difference in the world.

Sincerely,

Finola x

ABOUT FINOLA HOWARD

They're evil and manipulative. I just don't understand them and I hate that we have to put up with them. In fact, I'd love it if we just had nothing to do with them at all! These are the words I hear describing one of my best friends and I find myself constantly standing up for them. I keep saying no, no you're wrong. You just don't understand them. They just want to help you and get you to see yourself for who you really are. Like me, they think you're brilliant and they want to introduce you to your best customers but you just keep resisting them.

This is, of course, my dear friend "marketing". I love marketing. I always have. I don't experience that bad side of it. That kind of marketing is a lie and to me marketing is all about truth. The lies always get found out in the end anyway.

Early on in my career I crafted this phrase "Marketing is Your Truth Told. Great Marketing is Your Truth Shared" because there's always two key milestones on this journey. The first is to be brave enough, no matter the size of your business, to tell your truth. The truth of who you are and what you are trying to achieve. The next step is the market's response. When they like what you're saying, it'll resonate and they'll share it with the world. It'll never be shared unless it connects with someone, preferably paying customers.

I've always been a marketer. My first business was at age twelve when I was the CEO of our small hanging basket business for the mini company program in school. I learned how to do macrame and taught our 25 strong workforce of fellow students how to make them of a consistent quality. We cracked production early on and the chattier students (me), sold the baskets to every gift shop in the city. Everyone invested a Punt (Old Irish Pound) and at the end of the four months, we all got One Hundred Punts profit back. That was a lot of money for a twelve-year-old back then!

I have to say I loved how that felt. Having an idea, bringing it to life and making money from it. I also liked that we all made money from it. Everyone got the same share of the profits. We simply couldn't imagine it any other way. It didn't even come up for discussion.

My career has allowed me to see how every part of a business connects and contributes to its success. The variety has shown me that the patterns are not confined to industry or size of business. I worked in marketing roles for IIR, the world's largest conferencing company in London and New York and for MRI, the world's largest manage-ment recruitment agency in California. I headed up an ini-tiative to commercialise the construction division of the State Rail Authority in Sydney and developed an internal marketing strategy to promote company law services to the tax and accountancy divisions of KPMG in Dublin. I worked in a blended accountancy and marketing con-sultancy in the Irish midlands where I first got to work with small and medium sized businesses, ran a success-ful web design agency and an image licensing business. I have fond memories of century old books from the early printed books department of Trinity College Dublin and seeing how they could be brought to life again and gener-ate revenue for this revered university.

There are so many stories and lessons from each of these experiences and my work now taps into all of that. It's always about going deeper to unlock the truth behind a business. It's there you find the nuggets of uniqueness. That's the gold that transforms a business and makes it successful. That's how great marketing works! That's how I work.

If you'd like to tap into the unique gold in your business then reach out and say hello at www.finolahoward.com. I'd like to hear your story and help the market share it alongside you.

ACKNOWLEDGEMENTS

I didn't know I would fall in love with marketing and entrepreneurship until my sister Michelle discovered it first and said this feels a little like you Finola. Why don't you try this? My specific style of marketing is inspired by something I observed in my Dad when I was really young. I used to watch him as he truly listened to people and their stories. Often, he would have heard them before from someone else but you'd never know. He greeted each one with generosity and interest. What he listened for was the difference in each, their unique perspective and it always resulted in him getting the fuller picture of every scenario. And my Mum has always been the champion of getting it done. When the way is clear just go for it.

To the thousands of entrepreneurs who I have had the honour of working with. You inspire me to do this work so you can do yours and make your difference in the world. Keep going. Keep teaching me too. I grow so much from our journey together. To the people I work with and collaborate with on a regular basis to make it happen I thank you specifically Lucy, Aisling, Bren, Megan and many other experts in this space.

My book writing team made this book so possible. I sat on the idea of a book for so long. It wasn't meant to be until we came together. Debs, your process is incredible. I am amazed at how we have all written something we are proud of. We have laughed and cried together on this journey Rachel Evers, Sally Murphy and Emma Williams – next stop Italy! Thanks to Lisa de Caux for your heartfelt edits that encouraged me to keep going and to Jayr Cuario for sticking with it until it was right – thank you.

I am blessed to be surrounded by an amazing support network. Kevin and Sean, you are my everything. You never stop believing. To those I share my journey with Lucy, Maryann, Becky, Stephanie, Ula you each inspire me in so many ways, it would take another book to explain it.

And to the sea, I say thank you for showing me what freedom looks like. See you tomorrow!

WHAT'S NEXT?

If you like the idea that great marketing is all about nurturing the truth that's inside you, seeing how every part of your business connects to tell that story in practical, actionable ways then I'd love you to dig deeper with me. There are many ways you can do that and I'm present in each one.

You can take one of my courses. Some are evergreen so you can do things at your own pace there. Others are guided group programs that I run once a year. They are deeply transformative and you will share the space with others on the journey just like you. Laughter is a big part of how I work so I think you'll enjoy the space even when it challenges you.

Know this, whatever the course or program you choose I will answer every question and show you a way through every fear. You never need to be stuck because you will never be alone.

When you're ready for more you can join SOAR. When you soar you are increasing your reach, the "height" of your growth in a way that allows you to maintain that height and still leave you with the energy to imagine what's next.   It's a membership program that's about applying knowledge, deeper conversations and testing out new ideas; yours and what's happening in the marketplace.   It's about belief and support and the desire to achieve together as individuals. You still take the journey alone but never without someone to cheer you on. Every voice is important, every challenge and every opportunity. There are no limits here.

We can work together one to one. I only take on clients that have been referred, are on my contacts list and I think are a good match. Our work together is deeply personal whether it's just you or your whole team. We dive into the parts of the business that need attention and probably where you least expect. That requires bravery on all our parts and yet always in kindness. There is ease in this approach too. The outcome is always about next level growth whatever your starting point.

Get in touch at: www.finolahoward.com

MORE PRAISE FOR WHAT IF?

I loved reading this book. It was like having a mentor sitting at my shoulder telling me all the things that I need to hear. I felt each chapter spoke to me directly. The author's words are exactly what I need to read/hear at this early stage of my new business. In the final chapter the author said she has grown from writing it and that she is different because of it. I feel the very same, and already plan on rereading so that I can nurture this feeling and use it to help me grow into the new, more expansive version of me.

Dr Sarah Kelly,
Co-Founder Herology: The Science of Her

This book brings you into the crux of finding and unleashing your greatest power and joy as a business owner. No other book in its genre has brought me faster to the answers I was seeking so I could do my best work. Finola guides us with compassion and encourages us to be vulnerable enough to see how brave we are. If you're truly ready to tackle what really matters and what really brings you joy in your work and life, as well as realise that dream financially, read this book today, now.

Elaine Rogers, The Smart OBM

'What If?' is no ordinary book. It's a love letter to that part deep inside of us that yearns for expansion. The book felt so connected that, at times, I wasn't sure if I was hearing the voice of Finola or the whispers of my own soul. A beautifully written book that I will revisit again and again. Because that's the thing about expansion. It's an ongoing process. If we allow it to be.

Marina Branigan,
Operations Partner for Brilliant Consultants and Coaches

If you rolled your eyes when you read the title, this book is for you. Insightful, illuminating and refreshingly honest, it's a fresh and well-informed take on the ingredients for a business that's successful in every sense. (Which might not be what you think!). Although it's a short read, it's not a quick fix. It's a book to ponder on, consider and revisit. And when you start applying the lessons to your life and business, you'll see why it's worth leaving space for the next step to unfold. This book is a manual of possibility, firmly grounded in practicality and pragmatism. Read it when you're ready to stop thinking about 'What's next?' for your business and start asking, 'What if?'

Sarah Hanstock,
Content & Communications to Amplify Your Business Story

This book is challenging in the most gentle and encouraging way. Finola leads you on an important path to uncover your own truth. This book is all about you but Finola shares just enough about herself and her own vulnerability to show that she gets it and she gets you. This is a book you will want to keep and reread regularly to keep asking what if and stay aligned to your truth.

Susannah Simmons, Author, Helping Small Businesses
Take Care of their Customers and Themselves

Wow, there are so many beautiful words of wisdom and advice in this book for any entrepreneur; whether you're just starting out, scaling or already hugely successful. As a business owner currently grappling with the 'what ifs' and 'why nots' that come with scaling, I found this book to not only be insightful and practical but also quite emotional. Finola has such a beautiful way of getting you to lean into your potential, almost giving you permission to think big and design the business of your dreams. I'm sure I'll find myself coming back to this book again and again as it's like a beautiful compass guiding you to your North Star.

Lucy O'Reilly, Digital Strategy, Branding & Web Designer

It's a business book written by a human being who has looked through the rearview mirror with more wisdom and kindness. An insightful and refreshing perspective on business that highlights kindness and joy as essential parts of our everyday lives. It's a book I will keep returning to, like an old friend.

Heather McGuire
Integrative Health & Culinary Medicine Consultant & Speaker

Choosing to take the path of running my own business has been one of the biggest journeys of my life - freeing, fulfilling and at times, bewilderingly terrifying. The worst parts have been the moments when I have felt all alone, lost and unsure about how to take the next step forward and to where. This exquisitely crafted book means that no-one ever has to feel that way again.

As a seasoned and successful business owner, mentor and community builder, Finola has blazed a red lipped trail and now stands, arms outstretched, ready to take you by the hand so that you can climb to a better place where the view is breathtaking and the air is sweet to breathe. This book is a map, it is a manifesto and it is an essential companion for every person brave enough to listen to their own 'what if?' whisper.

Sally Murphy,
Author, TEDxwomen Speaker, Business Storyteller

Finola's book is a treasure, standing out by its raw, vulnerable journey into the heart of personal and professional growth. Through her candid sharing, she not only illuminates her own path but also reflects our vulnerabilities, encouraging us to embrace our unique voices and stories. Her wisdom, paired with practical advice, addresses the rollercoaster ride of pursuing one's purpose in our professional lives, highlighting the importance of listening to our inner whispers and the power of recognising our 'too muchness' as a marker of our inherent potential.

What truly sets Finola's work apart is her unwavering belief in the power of joy as the foundation of success. I felt her encouraging presence with every word, guiding me to find safety, empowerment, and notably, joy in the process of self-discovery and growth. She challenges us to prioritise our happiness, to find joy in our unique paths, and to pursue our dreams with courage and determination. Finola's message is clear: joy is not just a fleeting feeling but a crucial element of a fulfilling life and career.

Finola's book is more than a guide; it's a heartfelt invitation to step into the light, embrace our entirety, and share our truths. 'Will you join me?' she asks. The response, after delving into this transformative narrative, is a profound 'Yes.' Let's courageously define our own success and inspire others to discover their paths, contributing to a world enriched by our collective authenticity.

Rachel Evers,
Legal Counsel & Director of Legal Affairs at the
International Organization for Migration (IOM) |
Author of 'Your Personal Quest'

This is a book for every entrepreneur/business owner who has a sneaking - maybe even a big or inescapable - feeling that they've much more potential but aren't quite sure what the next step looks like. Finola's What If? is that next step.

This is a book that pulls no punches. It's human, real and true. Finola is a fantastical hybrid of the mentor you never knew you needed and the BFF you wish you had. She sees your potential yet calls you out when you sell yourself short. She draws attention to your ambition and capacity, yet makes it clear that 'success is not a passive endeavour.' So, this is a book filled with action. Finola first invites you and then takes you on a journey towards success - YOUR very own version of success. A success that you choose, and that you build yourself, with your 'Unique Ability' at the heart of it. A success fuelled by purpose (again, your unique purpose) and underpinned by values. No-one can decide what that looks like except you.

Best of all, it's a success that is defined by joy - where the joy you get in and from your work becomes the key metric. Where joy is a commercial decision. Where 'growth doesn't have to be hard - it can come with ease.'

So, if you feel stuck or a little uncertain about where to begin to get to the next level of success, this book is for you. Not only will it bring a smile to your face (and your neck will ache from all the nodding in recognition), but you'll come away with a clear map for how to 'Expand into YOU.' What's better than that?

Gillian Fallon,
Writing for Thought Leaders, Scale Ups and C Suite Executives

Every now and again, a book like 'What If?' comes along to truly make a difference. Through Finola's distinct voice, this book offers wisdom and practical guidance, resonating deeply with the reader. The concept of 'hear the whisper' is a highlight, urging readers to listen to their inner guidance. It inspires the reader to undertake THE WORK that truly matters to them. Finola's book promises to be a transformative road map for anyone wanting to cultivate a successful business and personal life. This book will help you become unstuck, no matter where you find yourself on your business journey.

Rachel Gotto,
Midlife Crisis Coach, Clinical Hypnotherapist,
Bestselling Author, TEDx Speaker

Author Finola Howard is The Entrepreneur Whisperer. Her powerful words tend your heart, mind and soul, daring you to lift the lid on your potential. Through a series of truth seeking questions and an alchemical toolkit, you'll be popped out of your comfort zone to where the joy is in your life and business. This book holds a mirror up to what is possible and shows you that you are worth your weight in gold.

Frea O'Brien,
Business Numerologist

Have you ever asked yourself what you are for? 'What If?' is for anyone who has and would like to change what they are doing professionally as a result. It is a guide that helps you delve into yourself and find your values and purpose so that you and your business are aligned. You should find joy in what you do because building a business is serious graft. If you are aligned and you get joy from your work, you are more likely to work in a balanced way and more likely to succeed. Finola provides the tools to work out your values, your purpose and how you can measure the joy you will get from your venture before you spend loads of time doing it.

My business partner and I said to each other at the outset of Untapped that it should be fun otherwise we will stop. But we never measured 'fun'. Finola's Joy Compass helps you measure it and keep it in mind throughout the journey.

This book aims to help you prioritise yourself above everything else. I am a father of 6 children, prioritising myself has just never been possible. As a founder, I never prioritised myself either. I read somewhere that you should always pay yourself first, this jarred with me so much, I always paid myself last! Prioritising myself will take a serious mindshift. The exercises in this short book aim to help me make that mindshift. Each step in the book is threaded with Finola's personal stories and challenges along her career and personal life, giving context to each exercise and bringing them to life. This book is a quick read but worth reviewing again and again to ensure you are prioritising yourself in your life - a recipe for success.

Brendan O'Hara,
Co-Founder & CTO Untapped AI

What if there was a book that saw you as you really are as a business owner?

What if it saw your hopes, dreams, and fears?

What if it spoke to those hopes, dreams, and fears, recognised them, and answered them?

That's what Finola Howard has achieved with her book 'What if?'

The introduction begins the conversation with the reader by asking 'what if you are my one reader?' That conversation continues throughout the book as the reader is gently invited to 'hear the whisper' and 'feed the whisper' of their dreams.

I love that 'what if?' is such a broad question. The reader is free to fill in the blank of what success is to them. There's a recognition that not every business owner wants to hit a six figure income, and that's ok. Because the essential elements in achieving the success you want are to have purpose, joy and make the money you need to make it happen.

Finola guides you through each step of the way, with lots of examples to bring the theory to life.

This is a short book, but that doesn't mean you will get through it quickly! Allow time to sit with the ideas and work through the suggestions. Because what if this was the book you were waiting for to bring your business to the next level?

Maureen McCowen, Soft Skills Success

Finola's book is a beacon of inspiration and wisdom. From the opening paragraphs, she speaks directly to our fears and desires, inviting us on a journey of self-discovery and empowerment. Her emphasis on joy as a powerful indicator of success as well as her practical tools and personal anecdotes, make her book a transformative read. I feel inspired and uplifted, ready to embrace life and entrepreneurship with renewed enthusiasm and purpose.

Mary Ann McGowan,
Leadership Development Trainer,
Coach, Speaker and Author

A must-read gem for entrepreneurs. 'What If?' is a beautifully written treasure trove of wisdom for entrepreneurs in any field. It's not just another business book—it's a practical guide that's easy to understand and apply to your own life and work.

In clear and simple language, Finola shares valuable insights on how to regain control when life feels overwhelming. Whether you're struggling with the pressures of a busy work life or simply seeking more balance and joy, this book offers practical advice that anyone can benefit from.

A must-read for anyone looking to find happiness and fulfilment in both their professional and personal lives. It's a breath of fresh air in the world of business literature, offering a much-needed reminder that success is about more than just work—it's about finding harmony and joy in all aspects of life.

Rachel Doyle, Author & Founder of Arboretum 5 Star
Garden & Lifestyle Centres

This book is simple, engaging, innovative, motivational, and emotional. This is no little book! I cried through the first few pages, not sure who I was crying for exactly Finola or me! It stirred me up, I want to have a go at this work. Well done, for your bravery, Finola, superb.

Regina Curley, Author and Life Coach

With a profound pivot away from success as society defines it, 'What If?' lights a path towards joy as the true compass. Finola's vulnerability is a rhythmic drumming that emerges as the heart of the book, showcasing how authenticity can lead us to redefine success – where joy is not simply a measure but a method of success, with financial gain as its natural consequence, not its primary goal.

Brent Perkins,
Speaker/Author/Coach – Championing a Life Lived
by Choice, Not by Chance | Founder at 3xBold

In 'What If?' Finola opens up a multi-layered box, laid out with an assortment of beautiful and well used tools, nuts and bolts to co-construct ideas around success and fulfilment with every reader individually.

Through a series of introspective provocations, she delves into fundamental questions about passion, purpose, and the embodiment of joy. Challenging us to redefine and make personal meaning of our realities, work and success.

By juxtaposing personal anecdotes with practical tasks and metrics, she nudges readers to reflect on their aspirations, confront fears, and chart a course towards a more meaningful and purpose-driven life. 'What If?' is not a book; it's a treasure-map for anyone seeking to navigate their potential.

While this takes you on a journey of self-discovery and empowerment, each page resonates with her deep understanding of human psychology, enterprise curation, design thinking and her commitment to fostering continued learning and holistic growth.

Finola's practice orients us to the transformative power of authenticity.

Tasneem Khan, Founding Partner EARTHCoLab

Finola's 'What if?' book could not be more different - it is thought-provoking, asks the right questions that each of us must answer for ourselves, and shows that there is a different way than before. That you can prioritize yourself first, that you can find fulfilment in your career with joy in it, that it is possible to have a sense of mission at work and not neglect other areas of life, that you can have purpose and balance together. I am grateful she decided to write this, I could not wait to read it. And right now, I need to sit down and reflect on all these questions and then implement the model she created.

Izabela Chaber-Lipecka,
Global Director of Growth, Software One

If you want to up your game in your business, this is the book to read. Finola Howard uses her own lived experience, as well as her extensive experience in working with clients on their marketing, to help you get clear on: defining success on your terms; your purpose; finding your voice; bringing more joy to your work; and making the money you deserve. No matter your stage in business, if you find yourself 'stuck' in some way, read this book - it will inspire you like it has inspired me.

Aoife O'Brien, Founder Happier At Work

'What If?' has left a significant mark on my perspective towards both life and business. At the heart of this book is the Joy/ Release Compass, a unique tool that elegantly brings together the core themes of joy, release, purpose, and personal fulfilment. It's a compass that doesn't just point north but inward, guiding readers towards a deeper understanding of what truly matters.

The book is punctuated with powerful one-liners that act as emotional checkpoints, stopping you in your tracks. More than once, I found these simple yet profound statements stirring something deep within me, bringing tears (I'll admit it!) and realisations that have shifted my outlook on personal and professional growth. It felt like having Finola Howard herself sitting across from me, her voice clear and resonant, speaking directly to my soul. Her ability to connect through her writing is extraor-dinary, making the experience not just about reading, but about feeling seen, heard and understood.

For anyone at a crossroads, looking for a sign, or simply in search of joy in their work, "What If?" offers a path to clarity and a reminder that the journey to fulfilment is as much about releasing what doesn't serve us as it is about embracing our true selves. Finola Howard doesn't just write; she reaches out, transforming her readers with every page.

Debbie Jenkins, founder, author, publisher

This book has it all – actionable steps, stories told with authen-ticity and honesty, probing questions, and lots of home truths. It is a very practical book; yes, the theory is there but what struck me most is that it contained so many practical steps and actions that can be taken immediately. "What If?" is well laid out and easy to follow. Finola's concept of 'hear', 'feel' and 'feed' the whisper is genius. As I was going through each section, my anticipation of what the next whisper held was growing and ultimately, the whisper transforming to a roar was a powerful metaphor. The book is very relatable with real life scenarios, challenges, and blockages. The 'what if section' had my own mind wandering, dreaming, and finishing these sentences with many what if's I hadn't previously considered. What a great read! This is a must read for all entrepreneurs whether starting out, changing direction or taking your business to the next level.

Catriona Kirwan, Executive & Life Coach

From the first page of the book, I felt goosebumps all over my body. It was my soul trying to scream my truth, my Purpose. In her joyful and genius book Finola Howard guides you to your own, unique success. Through ups and downs of this journey, through dark valleys of fears, all the way to your Truth. She can spot and call out your fears so precisely, she names them for you, to bring them to your awareness. This way you can dissolve or transform them, which allows you to make that first step, and then the second and then you just start walking. Towards your joyful success.

"What If?" is both deep and easy to read. This book made my purpose flourish and finally kick start my ideas into action!.

Ula Banasik, People & Culture Leader | Creating great and effective work environments where people can focus on meaningful work | Remote work excellence | HR Digitalization | Advisor | Mentor

This is a book for anyone who needs a compass to steer their entrepreneurial or personal journey. It is an honest depiction of what is needed to enable and foster growth. A thoroughly enjoyable and insightful read. This book made me want to cry, hug Finola for writing it and change all at once. A truly thought evoking and provoking read.

Miriam O'Hara, Senior Recruitment Manager | Driving Global Talent for Strategic Business Growth, Mace Consultancy Ireland Ltd

Although entrepreneur-focused "WHAT IF" is not just a business book, it's a compelling self-help book that delves into the power of positive thinking, a must-read for young and old in all walks of life. Through a combination of her own experiences, anecdotes, quotes, and practical advice, Finola encourages us to think big, understand our purpose, embrace gratitude, and align actions to core values in order to be successful in life. This book serves as a motivational guide that inspires readers to harness the power of their thoughts and beliefs to create a more fulfilling and abundant life. I'll be sharing it with my kids!

David Walsh, Executive Chairperson Halocare Group,
Founder Netwatch

Being in the depths of a solo entrepreneurship journey I can confidently say that Finola's authentic approach has captured the essence of this journey in her book. I thoroughly enjoyed the personable accounts and her relatable insights. Each page invites you to slow down, absorb, and reflect on the depth of the strategies. Whether you're just starting out or seeking to up your business game, this book is a beacon of guidance and inspiration.

Norma O'Kelly, Systemic Coach Focused on Delivering
Creative Change in Life and in Work for Leaders, Teams
and Individuals who want to go deeper | Systemic
Wellness | Nurturing Belonging in Team Dynamics

When we get to the end of our lives and look back what will we say about the life that we have lived. Will we have left it too late to wonder what if then? Finola's book "WHAT IF" allows us to the take the lid off the perceived obstacles that are preventing us from achieving true joy and freedom! By sharing her own challenges and experiences we are encouraged to embrace our uniqueness, to become more self aware, to be spontaneous, to embrace vulnerabilities, to move out of our comfort zones, to step up and be accountable to ourselves. Finola reminds me of the commercial importance of my business and that financial freedom brings choice, excitement, purpose, community and growth. I would highly recommend this book. I look forward to giving myself permission to be curious and adventurous with all my What If's. You never know all my dreams might come true!

Teresa O'Shea,
Transformational Life & Business Coach

"What if" is not just a book about marketing strategies; it's an exploration into the Author Finola Howard and how she uses her remarkable intuitiveness, matched with her own life wisdom to help you find those golden nuggets that are deep inside, and to urge readers to harness change and challenges, as opportunities for personal growth. It feels, without a doubt like a real conversation you're having with Finola AND yourself. It's powerfully emotional and she takes you by the hand to softly bring you through it, hitting the right spots every time.

Deborah Jordan, Co-Founder Chuzeday – the Digital Community Marketplace

What if a book defies your expectations? Finola Howard's book "What If..." did just that, surprising me in the most delightful way. It's like a big, warm, comforting hug, urging you to be even more of who you are so that your business thrives and you find joy and financial success with ease.

The book surprised me because I had anticipated a marketing and business strategy book, an area in which Finola excels. She is pragmatic, insightful, and inspiring when working with and advising people in business. However, without personal growth, the possibility of achieving business success is often thwarted.

Finola powerfully addresses personal growth in this compelling book chock full of nuggets of wisdom. She makes practical, apparently simple suggestions to enable you to access your most effective self so that you and your business can thrive.

One of the suggestions I've committed to is writing five positive "What ifs…" to start my day, a practice that brings me joy and clarity. I'll explore so many more suggestions and ideas going forward. Thank you, Finola, for a powerful book I'll reread many times so that friction is gone and joy and growth move in.

Julie Silfverberg,
Empowering Coaches with Custom Web Design &
Branding Solutions

This book is written for all those people still trying to understand why they haven't started their own business yet or shaped the business they have in the way that works for them. I read it with Finola's voice in my head, telling me that I am on the right path because 'this version of success is not a destination or an "end point".' It starts with why I do what I do, and ends with wherever I want to take it and shape it the way that feels right for me. And Finola's book helped me be ok with my choice and allow success to grow in a space I create for myself. Thank you for holding my hand, Finola.

Hanna Laatio McDonnell, Outsourced Marketing Expert

In her book What If, Finola Howard guides the entrepreneur to understanding the weight that must be given to clarity around purpose - our why! Life gets cluttered as we get older when oftentimes we have always known our purpose we just needed it to be fed. That is the Magic of the Whisper in her book and the idea that "until you hear your inner voice clearly nobody is going to hear yours. Thanks for your generosity in sharing your knowledge Finola.

Olive Garde | Designer Kilcarrig Designs

I felt Finola has written this book especially for me and I enjoyed it immensely. Having had the pleasure of working with Finola in the past, I felt her calm voice and genuine passion for helping entrepreneurs on every single page. It is a book I will return to again and again to pull me back on track when I feel I'm getting swamped by the day to day operations of running my own business and I'm sure I will take away some new revelation each time I reread.

Mary Jennings, Author Founder of Forget The Gym: Go Outside. Get Moving. Feel Alive.

The content is brilliant in Finola's book "WHAT IF". I especially love the Hear Feel and Feed the whisper bits. We read stuff all the time and it's just information in and out. But they really do add to letting you hold onto how you feel about what you have read. It is very lifting. I, actually feel lifted after reading it. I look forward to having a signed copy in the studio to show off. :)

John Murray, John Murray Headshots

Empowering, uplifting and packed with loads of practical help- a great supportive read along your journey in life and one that will help you understand your purpose and take the steps to follow it.

Catherine O'Keefe,
Workplace Menopause Consultant

This book is therapy for your business. Whether you're starting out or at a standstill in your journey - this step by step guide will show you how to unlock your limiting thoughts and reach your full potential. It's a powerful read and really allowed me to pause, reflect, and move forward with ease. Joy is important and so is money!

Fatima Awan, Founder at FINIITE AI

www.ingramcontent.com/pod-product-compliance
Lightning Source LLC
Chambersburg PA
CBHW040924210326
41597CB00030B/5168